Abba Amma

Abba Amma

Improvisations on the Lord's Prayer

Nicola Slee

CANTERBURY
PRESS
Norwich

© Nicola Slee 2022

Published in 2022 by Canterbury Press
Editorial office
3rd Floor, Invicta House,
108–114 Golden Lane,
London EC1Y OTG, UK
www.canterburypress.co.uk

Canterbury Press is an imprint of Hymns Ancient & Modern Ltd
(a registered charity)

Hymns Ancient & Modern® is a registered trademark of
Hymns Ancient & Modern Ltd
13A Hellesdon Park Road, Norwich,
Norfolk NR6 5DR, UK

Scripture quotations are from New Revised Standard Version Bible:
Anglicized Edition, copyright © 1989, 1995 National Council of
the Churches of Christ in the United States of America. Used by
permission. All rights reserved worldwide.

British Library Cataloguing in Publication data

A catalogue record for this book is available
from the British Library

ISBN: 978-1-78622-321-0

Typeset by Regent Typesetting
Printed and bound by
CPI Group (UK) Ltd

For my parents, who have mediated divine love,
and will not now read this book.
For all the abbas and ammas who have prayed
for and with me from my birth.
For my godchildren, who call out my abba amma love.

Even if I have gone astray, I am your child, O God;
you are my father and mother.
Arjan, Sikh saint, died 1606

Who is my mother, who is my father? Only you, O God.
Kekchi Tribe, American-Indian

Both in Barbara Greene and Victor Gollancz, *God of a Hundred Names* (London: Hodder & Stoughton, 1962), p. 145.

Contents

Acknowledgements

If I were to attempt to name all those whose love and prayer have shaped my praying over many years and my living into the Prayer of Jesus, it would be a very long list. I attempted something like this in the Preface to *Praying Like a Woman*, and those deep debts of gratitude remain. Here, I will limit myself to a few remarks.

My parents have shaped my struggles in prayer as in life, in ways I seek to acknowledge in a number of places in this book, particularly Chapter 1. During the writing of this book, my elder brother, Ian, estranged from the family for decades, re-entered my life for a brief few months before his death. I have prayed for Ian my whole life long and very frequently railed against the apparent uselessness of my prayer, only to be surprised this past year by a reconciliation I could never have imagined. Towards the very end of the copy-editing process of this book, my father also died, yet the relationship with a parent does not end in death and may, in some ways, become deeper and freer. The love and solidarity of my two sisters, Sally-Ann and Jane, have come to mean more to me in recent years, as we are all ageing together and seeking to support one another even as we have sought to support, from a distance, our ageing parents. An underlying theme of this book is the changing nature of the journey of faith and prayer as we age.

Many abbas and ammas, godparents, spiritual grandparents and parents, as well as siblings in the community of faith, have prayed for and with me over many years – far too many to name. During the writing of this book, two beloved aunts – my father's sisters, Marjorie and Greta – died within a week of each other. Both have been important in my life, and my Auntie Marjorie in particular has been a life-long godmother (if not officially), praying faithfully for me, always interested in my life and work, always eager to meet and talk. A beloved spiritual mother, Sr Marie Watson, who birthed my first truly 'owned' faith as a teenager, died unexpectedly in February 2019. My sense of the presence and prayer of the community of saints 'on the other side' grows with each mortal loss. Others upon whose wisdom and prayer I rely, such as Donald Eadie and Sr Mary John Marshall OSB, are facing the diminishments of ageing with a courage and trust that teaches me daily.

I have missed being able to visit Glasshampton monastery and Malling Abbey during lockdown, yet I know that their prayer continues day in, day out. Simply knowing they are there is, itself, a great encouragement and source of strength. Colleagues and friends at Queen's and All Saints, Kings Heath, have continued to be 'with me' and support me in so many ways, if largely in physical absence during much of the past two years. Among many other creative folk who make up the community of All Saints, Gillian and Jake Lever are two fine artists whose work graces our home, and I am delighted to have one of Gillian's beautiful abstracts to form the cover of this book. With its cool, harmonious colours, its gorgeous textures and its sense of openings into vistas and depths beyond, it repays close and disciplined attention and gifts the viewer with unexpected resonances and new connections on each viewing.

A handful of people have had a closer involvement in shaping this book, reading it and offering their wisdom, insights and creative suggestions – all of which have made it a better book than it otherwise would have been. My editor at Canterbury Press, Christine Smith, has been unfailingly patient as deadline after deadline has been missed and renegotiated, not only because of the peculiar circumstances imposed by Covid but more significantly due to the deaths, illnesses and increasing frailty of members of my family during the writing of this book. She never once made me feel bad about the missed deadlines, offering empathic concern and good suggestions in equal measure. Rachel Geddes has done a fabulous, efficient and careful copy-edit of the book, and I am also grateful for her care and thoughtfulness in the process.

Ashley Cocksworth and Hannah Brookes, fine theologians

and teachers, both read the manuscript and, from their different areas of expertise and lived experience, offered many suggestions that have enriched the text and cheered me on through the stops and starts of the project. Their daughter, Lucy May, born during lockdown, whom I have yet to meet, has also woven her presence into this book, not only in the one place where she is mentioned (p. 139), but also in my growing sense of the courage and faith that is going to be required by her and those of her generation as they grow up in a world facing the increasing effects of climate change. As so many of those who came before me have sustained me and held my life through its many vicissitudes by their prayer and witness, so I commit to pray for the ones who are coming after me, which includes my nieces and nephews – Fay, Imogen and James Lydden, Cara and Frankie Hadwick – and my beloved godchildren, both official and adopted – John James Featherby, Nathalie Richards, Hannah Skinner, Tom Sudbury and Morven Cameron, Jelly Morgans and Stephen Canning, as well as those like Lucy May Cocksworth who are so young as to seem like grand-godchildren, if such a thing exists! Although I cannot envisage the world Lucy is going to grow into, I do know that the prayer which has sustained centuries of the faithful will continue to hold her life and the lives of all those coming behind me.

Alison Woolley, originally one of my doctoral students and now a good friend, a skilled writer and spiritual guide to many, also read the manuscript, paying attention to detail as well as the bigger picture and shape of the whole. The quality of her attention – something she brings to her prayer as well as her work and her relationships with others – enabled me to notice things in my own work which required more attention and thus to better them. Stephen Burns has been unfailingly encouraging and enthusiastic about this writing project and, once again, has blessed me with his prodigious theological and liturgical knowledge, pointing me to texts and ideas I might very well otherwise have missed. He is also a faithful praying presence in my life; I am glad I was able to share some of the first Abba Amma prayers with Stephen and some of his students at Pilgrim Theological College, Melbourne, when I was privileged to be a guest of the College on sabbatical in autumn 2019 and receive their insights as they prayed the prayers. Rosie Miles, my first reader and most accomplished literary critic, never lets me get away with sloppy writing or easy theology and has brought a fierce and assured editorial eye to every piece in this book, improving many as a result. At the same time, her smiley faces and ticks littered liberally throughout the manuscript helped me to believe there was something worth persevering with. Every one of these readers has prayed the prayers with me, as well as bringing the richness of their own wide-ranging learning and scholarship to the text, and I am deeply grateful for the care they have taken over my work.

And how can I fail to mention our two cats, Tinker and Pumpkin, in this litany of thanksgiving? They have been even more significant presences than usual throughout the writing of this book, because we have all spent so much more time at home, in house and garden, than at any previous time in our shared lives. The cats, like us, are getting older and Pumpkin, in particular, like me, now lives with a number of health conditions which require quantities of medication and a special diet. They are frail, mortal beings, even as we are, and who knows how much longer they will share their lives with us? While they do, their uncompromising feline trust in the humans with whom they share their lives is its own gift, offering a parable of prayer we daily witness and participate in.

Introduction

Source

Amma Abba: source from whom I came.
I reverence your name.

Your own beloved child,
may I be bold

to work for your kindom
on earth as in heaven.

I know my failure to care for my neighbour –
my sister, father, mother, brother.

You will forgive from your bountiful store
providing my needs, neither less nor more.

Out of the largesse of your grace,
give us all a place

at your overflowing table.
Feed us, that we may become able

to quieten our hungers,
attend to others, both near ones and strangers.

May we so linger in love
at your banquet – no hurry to move –

until we are filled with your joy
rising within and between us – pure, unalloyed.

Of whose family we are

Abba Amma
of whose family we are

Holy, holy, holy
your unnameable, numberless names

your kindom come
your living will be done

here and now, today
in us, this place, this unrepeatable world

as it is in the aeons of aeons
and the splendour of heaven

Give us today a hunger for your living bread
and joy in breaking and sharing it

Make us see how we squander your gifts
and, seeing, mend your image in us

Defend us from our self-destructive ways
And protect us from the evil of hate

Yours is the ever-flowing, everlasting
life and love and vitality

For now and for ever and ever. Amen.

The Prayer of Jesus – known by many Protestants as the Lord's Prayer and by Catholics as the Our Father or Pater Noster – is both a text and a prayer practice that connects Christians East and West, Catholic, Orthodox and Protestant, throughout time and eternity.[1] It is one of the most precious prayer texts to Christians because it at once unites us with the Prayer of Jesus and that of Christians throughout history as well as across the globe. As Stephen Cherry suggests, 'praying the Lord's Prayer will draw us into a deeper relationship with its originator, Jesus himself, as well as with the countless others who have used and reflected on the prayer.'[2] The gift of Jesus to his disciples, it encapsulates the heart of his teaching and, we may presume, his own prayer; we surely cannot imagine that Jesus would teach his disciples to pray in a way that was inimical to his own practice. As Leonardo Boff puts it, 'Here, we find a crystallization of the very essence of Jesus' experience and the basic landmark of his teachings.'[3] From Tertullian onwards, many have seen in the Lord's Prayer a summary or epitome, in condensed and prayed-form, of the whole gospel – *breviarium totius evangelii*, as Tertullian's Latin has it.[4]

This is a prayer which is, at one and the same time, profoundly simple and simply profound. No more than a few lines long, a child may memorize it in a few days and yet it is a prayer that can last a lifetime as one prays it in solidarity with saints and sinners down the ages and seeks to live into the just and loving relationships it calls into being: relationships that include the whole family of humanity as 'brother' and 'sister', as well as the nearer relationships of those we live with and struggle to love and forgive, grounded in the primary relationship with God, the Abba Amma of all.

---

1 A considerably shorter version of this introduction appears in *Fragments for Fractured Times: What Feminist Practical Theology brings to the Table* (London: SCM Press, 2020), chapter 2, and formed the basis of a talk to the Modern Church Conference in July 2017.

2 Stephen Cherry, *Thy Will Be Done: The 2021 Lent Book* (London: Bloomsbury, 2020), pp. 2–3.

3 Leonardo Boff, *The Lord's Prayer: The Prayer of Integral Liberation* (Maryknoll, NY: Orbis Books, 1983), p. 17.

4 Tertullian, 'On Prayer', which can be found in many versions online, for example, www.newadvent.org/fathers/0322.htm.

John Dominic Crossan describes it as 'a prayer from the heart of Judaism on the lips of Christianity for the conscience of the world', emphasizing that it does not belong only to Christians but can be – and is – prayed by many who identify, in some way, with the life and values of Jesus of Nazareth. He goes on to speak of it as 'a radical manifesto and a hymn of hope for all humanity in language addressed to all the earth', offering strong reasons for its enduring popularity.[5] Quite simply, it is 'the greatest prayer', although Crossan also describes it as 'Christianity's strangest prayer' for the paradoxes at its heart:

> It is prayed by all Christians, but it never mentions Christ. It is prayed in all churches, but it never mentions church. It is prayed on all Sundays, but it never mentions Sunday. It is called 'the Lord's Prayer', but it never mentions 'Lord'.[6]

As this quote from Crossan suggests, the Lord's Prayer is regarded by many as a universal rather than a partisan prayer, a prayer in which the pray-er aligns him or herself with all of humanity and not simply those who profess themselves as Christian. This is suggested partly by the form of address, which assumes a 'we' rather than an 'I': the prayer is addressed to 'our Father' not 'my Father', and asks for 'our daily bread' and forgiveness of 'our sins', not 'my' bread or sins. But it goes deeper than this. Daniel Migliore goes so far as to suggest that, in praying the Lord's Prayer:

> We pray as a community and on behalf of all humanity and, indeed, of all creatures. Not a trace of individualism is evident in this prayer. There is no search for personal salvation apart from the renewal of the life of the whole creation. The Lord's Prayer is thus a prayer not of individualistic piety but of solidarity in suffering and hope with the entire groaning creation.[7]

5 John Dominic Crossan, *The Greatest Prayer: Rediscovering the Revolutionary Message of the Lord's Prayer* (London: SPCK, 2011), p. 2.
6 Crossan, *The Greatest Prayer*, p. 1.
7 Daniel L. Migliore, Preface, in *The Lord's Prayer: Perspectives for*

As such, this is a prayer which is profoundly expressive of the mission and ministry of Jesus to save, heal and liberate human-kind. Thus, Henry French describes the Lord's Prayer as 'a primer on mission in the way of Jesus',[8] suggesting that:

> To pray this prayer is to stand in solidarity with all people who experience in their bodies, minds, and spirits the multi-farious oppressions of a world where God's name is not sanc-tified, where God's kingdom has not fully come, and where human wills resist the divine will. To pray this prayer is to join with Jesus, whose very life was a hallowing of God's name, who embraced and embodied the kingdom of God, and whose will was to do the will of his Father (John 4:34).

This is a point made powerfully by Leonardo Boff's study of the Lord's Prayer, which he regards as 'the prayer of integral liberation', prayed out of 'a time of crisis, of temptations, of decisions' in our own day, just as it was in Jesus', uniting the longing for heaven with the struggle for liberation on earth.[9]

While at once an utterly simple prayer, taught to and prayed by countless generations of children, the Prayer of Jesus has also been plumbed by the greatest minds of Christian tradition. Ash Cocksworth describes it as 'Christian theology's most prayed prayer'[10] and goes on to explore ways in which this prayer, and its primary pray-er, Jesus, have shaped Christian doctrine as well as practice, most profoundly. He explores the way in which this central prayer of Christianity is interpreted from the earliest tradition onwards and in the thinking of all the great theologians and saints of every age, including in contemporary times, when we find feminist, liberationist and

---

Reclaiming Christian Prayer, ed. Daniel L. Migliore (Grand Rapids, MI: Eerdmans, 1993), pp. 1–2.

8 Henry French, 'The Lord's Prayer: A Primer on Mission in the Way of Jesus', *Word & World* 22.1 (2002), pp. 18–26, https://wordand world.luthersem.edu/content/pdfs/22-1_Lords_Prayer/22-1_French.pdf (accessed 28.01.21).

9 Boff, *Lord's Prayer*, p. 17.

10 Ashley Cocksworth, *Prayer: A Guide for the Perplexed* (London: T&T Clark, 2018), p. 109.

postcolonial readings of the Lord's Prayer, among others.[11] Cocksworth gives examples of the ways in which the Lord's Prayer has inspired and given rise to a variety of treatments in preaching, literary works – such as poetry and literature – and been depicted in the visual arts. Although he does not include musical versions of the Lord's Prayer, one can think of countless examples of mass settings of the prayer by composers of every age and culture, as well as more popular renderings such as Cliff Richard's Millennial version, Charlotte Church's rendition of the 1935 Albert Malotte setting (also recorded by Barbara Streisand and Andrea Bocelli), Doyle Dykes's guitar version and various reggae and calypso versions – plus many, many more.[12]

* * *

Like many, I have prayed this prayer my entire life and it must be one of the earliest texts I learnt by heart. I am of a generation and from a rural community where all children were taught the prayer both at school and at church or Sunday school (I'm not sure if that is still the case). I am pretty sure we would have recited the Lord's Prayer (as I then called it) every day in school assembly, as well as every Sunday at the Methodist chapel up the road from our farm where I went to church with my family. I imbibed it, then, almost with my mother's milk, and it formed my earliest sense and understanding of faith and of prayer, as well as the bedrock of public worship, although I can't say this was a conscious thing. I don't think I ever gave the prayer any reflective consideration as a child or even, later, as a teenager when prayer became intensely real to me in the form of a deep, experiential love-bond between my soul and Jesus, my beloved Saviour. My own private prayer was something much more spontaneous and personal than any merely learnt prayer could be (or so I thought), forged in the intimate language of lovers.

---

11 See Cocksworth, *Prayer*, p. 112, footnote 8.

12 A quick search on YouTube brings up a huge range of musical settings of the Lord's Prayer.

I do remember, as a teenager, that calling God 'Abba' was a significant and precious thing, the fatherhood of God ranking close to the intense personal love of Jesus and the sense of the Holy Spirit as a living presence that were each at the heart of my relationship to God. It was only later, at university, where I read theology and studied the Gospel texts closely, that I came to reflect more consciously on the content of the prayer, reading Jeremias' classic works on the Abba-relationship of Jesus,[13] C. H. Dodd's studies of the parables of the kingdom[14] and other commentaries on and studies of the prayer practice of Jesus and the early Church. Then, I began consciously to recognize the richness of the content of the Lord's Prayer and to understand how it encapsulated the heart of Jesus' praxis and proclamation. At that stage, I simply accepted on trust the masculine form of address to God as Father, the monarchical language of kingdom and so on, that are part and parcel of the landscape of the prayer.

However, it was not long before my journey into feminism in general and feminist theology in particular began to challenge much of the taken-for-granted patriarchal and paternal language, imagery and theology of the Christian gospel as I had received it. While my formal studies contained nothing whatsoever on liberation or feminist theologies (indeed, barely any theologies from the modern era), I began to get involved in informal feminist groups and to read whatever I could lay my hands on about feminist theology and women's religious experience (very little indeed, in those heady days!). When I got my first job as a lecturer in theology and religious studies (at what was then the Roehampton Institute of Higher Education), one of the first courses I taught was a selection of classic texts in twentieth-century theology, which ranged from Barth, Bultmann and Bonhoeffer to Moltmann, Gutiérrez and Ruether (I added the last three to the existing syllabus). From

---

13 Joachim Jeremias, *The Lord's Prayer* (Philadelphia, PA: Fortress, 1964); *The Prayers of Jesus* (Philadelphia, PA: Fortress, 1978).

14 C. H. Dodd, *The Parables of the Kingdom* (Glasgow: Collins, 1978; first edition, 1935).

there, I began to develop courses dedicated to liberation and feminist theologies, ensuring that my own reading and learning developed apace as I taught others. While reading more deeply in liberation and feminist theologies (this was the early and mid-1980s), I began to get more involved in feminist-inspired liturgy groups in south-west London, where I was living at the time. This was the time of the St Hilda Community, which became well known after the Bishop of London threw the community out of St Benet's Chapel, where we had been meeting, and a collection of short essays about the life of the community was published with a selection of liturgical texts.[15] But there were other groups too, in which I was involved: a local liturgy group meeting in St Mark's Church, Wimbledon; an occasional liturgy group which met as part of Women in Theology (WIT); and Jim Cotter was producing much of his liturgical material at this time, as well as gathering a group of those seeking new and more adventurous ways of praying, both publicly and privately, in his Cairns network.[16]

Although I remained a faithful Anglican, attending both local parish church and the College Chapel at Whitelands (the Anglican college which, with Methodist Southlands, Catholic Digby Stuart and Froebel, made up the Roehampton Institute), I was experimenting more and more with new forms of praying, extending the range of gendered and other metaphors for God, as well as the acceptable forms and styles of language to and about God, pushing beyond polite Anglican formality to more impassioned forms of protest, proclamation and praise. Not only in the various feminist-inspired liturgical groups, but also on the Southwark Ordination Course (and later, the Aston Training Scheme in Birmingham), I found spacious environments for theological and liturgical exploration and experimentation. Language was not the only consideration in these groups and fora: feminists and others disenfranchised by traditional forms of theology and worship were exploring

---

15 The St Hilda Community, *Women Included: A Book of Services and Prayers* (London: SPCK, 1991).

16 See www.cottercairns.co.uk/.

the place of the body and the passions in thinking about, and relating to, God, and pushing for overt political engagement in theology and liturgy. During this period, and later on, when I moved to Birmingham (in 1993), I was writing many of my own liturgies, poems and prayers, and experimenting with a range of forms and voices in my writing and in more embodied practice (published initially in *Praying Like a Woman*, then in later texts such as *Doing December Differently*, co-edited with Rosie Miles; *The Book of Mary*, *The Edge of God*, co-edited with Stephen Burns and Michael Jagessar; and later again in *Seeking the Risen Christa*).

***

Interestingly, throughout this time of liturgical and theological ferment, I gave the Lord's Prayer little attention. Which is not to say I did not come across a fair number of alternative versions of the text and indeed, I was doubtless using some of these quite regularly. Of course, it is important to recognize that variation in the text of the Lord's Prayer is there from its very beginning, built into its warp and weft, we might say, encouraging plurality and improvisation in those who pray it (an idea to which I will return a little later). There is no one, authorized or definitive version of the Lord's Prayer, despite attempts by some to impose one. The New Testament contains two versions of the prayer, one in Matthew (Matthew 6.9–13) and one in Luke (Luke 11.2–4). While similar, there are noticeable differences between the two versions, not least in Luke's terser address to God as 'Father' in contrast to Matthew's 'Our Father in heaven', and Luke's omission of Matthew's third petition in the second half of the prayer, 'May your will be done'.[17] There are also subtle differences in some of the petitions, such as variations in the words for 'this day' (Matthew) or 'each day' (Luke) in the petition for daily bread.

---

17 Many commentators notice the twofold structure of the prayer in which two series of three petitions follow the opening address: the first three concerning God and God's will, the second three concerning human need – for bread, forgiveness and protection from evil.

Clearly, at the time of the compilation of the New Testament texts, different versions of the prayer were circulating in different communities. The Didache, a short early Christian teaching document generally dated to the first century, contains a third version of the Lord's Prayer and instructs Christians to pray the prayer three times a day, suggesting that repeated daily praying of the Lord's Prayer was well established by the time of its composition. The version in the Didache (8.2)[18] is more or less the same as the version in Matthew. Though scholars may regard one or other of these versions as closer to Jesus' original usage, Bruce Chilton suggests we do better not to think of one fixed form of the prayer that Jesus always used, but rather a *pattern* or outline of prayer that very likely varied in its detail but retained core features and a recognizable shape.[19]

Variety and plurality in translations and paraphrases of the Lord's Prayer have continued unabated since the earliest New Testament times.[20] Every fresh translation of the Bible produced its own versions of the Lukan and Matthean texts, in the various languages and idioms of the world, far too many to consider here. Liturgical committees in different denominations have also produced their own variations, and this is reflected in different denominational versions of the prayer. Language used for the petition for forgiveness varies around 'debts' and 'trespasses', for instance; some churches favour, 'Do not bring us to the time of trial' over 'Do not lead us into temptation',

---

18 The Didache can be found online in a variety of translations, for example www.thedidache.com (in a somewhat archaic translation) and www.newadvent.org/fathers/0714.htm (in a more contemporary idiom).

19 Bruce Chilton, *Jesus' Prayer and Jesus' Eucharist: His Personal Practice of Spirituality* (Valley Forge, PA: Trinity Press International, 1997), pp. 26–7.

20 We could say exactly the same about the understanding and interpretation of the Lord's Prayer, which has been different in every age, context and situation. See Curtis Rose (ed.), *The Lord's Prayer: A Collection of Historical Writings on the Lord's Prayer* (Castle Rock, CO: reNEW publications, 2014) and Kenneth W. Stevenson, *The Lord's Prayer: A Text in Tradition* (London: SCM Press, 2004).

and so on. Protestant usage tends to add the doxology while the Roman churches generally do not.

Modern versions of the prayer are legion, prompted both by the desire to convert biblical language into more contemporary styles and idioms (as in *The Message*,[21] for example, or *The Street Bible*[22]) and by the felt need to paraphrase some of the original patriarchal and monarchical images and metaphors within the prayer (for example, in versions by Jim Cotter, Janet Morley and many others, to which I turn below).[23] Feminists began to object to the paternalism and patriarchal power associated with language of God as Father and to seek for alternative forms of address; similarly, the monarchical assumptions of kingdom language – expressed both in the petition, 'your kingdom come' and reinforced in the doxology at the end, which ascribes 'power, kingdom and glory' to God – are rejected by many. Gail Ramshaw describes as 'the myth of the crown' the hierarchical, monarchical and patriarchal world view assumed for centuries in Christendom, which depicted divine power in terms of ruling male elites, thereby placing women, children, non-dominant males and other marginalized persons at the bottom of the power pyramid.[24] From the 1960s onwards, individuals, networks and liturgical groups began to experiment with different versions and forms of the Lord's Prayer, taking on a wide range of literary styles and forms as well as introducing new imagery and symbolism. Some of these

---

21 Eugene H. Peterson, *The Message: The Bible in Contemporary Language* (New York: NavPress, 2002).

22 Rob Lacey, *The Street Bible* (Grand Rapids, MI: Zondervan, 2003).

23 John Henson's *Good as New: A Radical Retelling of the Scriptures* (Washington and Winchester: O Books, 2004; New Testament only) combines a concern for inclusive and expansive language with an informal, everyday style and idiom (using nicknames for many of the characters, for example 'Rocky' for Peter, as well as employing the feminine gender throughout for the Spirit).

24 Gail Ramshaw, *God Beyond Gender* (Minneapolis, MN: Fortress, 1995), p. 59.

prayers stick closely to the biblical originals, whereas others range much more widely and freely in their experimentation. Some have clearly been created for formal liturgical use, while others presuppose more intimate, personal settings of prayer.

To mention only a few more well-known examples, Jim Cotter created an expansive version of the Lord's Prayer in the first version of his *Prayer at Night*.[25] This version, which begins 'Life-giver, Pain-bearer, Love-maker' (with or without a preliminary 'Eternal Spirit'), became very widely used in Anglican and alternative liturgical circles in the 1970s and 1980s and was eventually adopted by the Anglican Church of New Zealand, with most of Jim's *Prayer at Night*, in its office of Night Prayer in the 1989 Prayer Book (and similarly by the Uniting Church in Australia's *Uniting in Worship 2*).[26] Although this is by far the best-known of Jim's versions of the Lord's Prayer, it is not the only one. It sits alongside three others, what Jim calls 'unfolding(s) of the Lord's Prayer', in his prayerbook, *Out of the Silence ... Into the Silence: Prayer's Daily Round*,[27] set in different forms, for different voices,

25 First published in a small gold paperback in 1983 before the advent of Cairns Publications, *Prayer at Night* went through numerous editions in small and larger versions, hardback and softback, with more or less expansive additions. What remained constant throughout was the original version of the Lord's Prayer, p. 56 of the 1983 edition.

26 The Anglican Church in Aotearoa, New Zealand and Polynesia, *A New Zealand Prayer Book* (Auckland: William Collins, 1989), p. 181 – though note that Jim's 'Love-maker' is lost and changed to the more anodyne 'Life-giver'; Stephen Burns informs me that only the Uniting Church in Australia's *Uniting in Worship 2* maintains the original address (and no official prayer book has kept Jim's gorgeous 'My unicorn' as part of his opening invocation: 'O Thou, Most Holy and Beloved, my Companion, my Unicorn, my Guide upon the Way'). I have always felt indignant on Jim's behalf that, while Anglicans the other side of the world were willing to welcome his liturgical creativity into their prayer books, the Church of England largely shunned his gifts, at least during most of his life. Finally in 1993, the revised Franciscan *Celebrating Common Prayer: A Version of the Daily Office* (London: Mowbray) included versions of Jim's Benedictus, Magnificat and Lord's Prayer, as well as prayers and canticles by Janet Morley.

27 Harlech: Cairns, 2006, pp. 505–10.

offering rich meditation on the theology and imagery of the prayer. These are not so much translations or paraphrases as discursive, meditative ruminations on the prayer. Much as I love them, they are too wordy for everyday use unless one has plenty of time and silence in which to sit with the words and phrases. As part of a regular diet of daily prayer, I'd turn elsewhere. Lala Winkley has a short, plain version addressed to 'God, lover of us all, most holy one', from Greenham Common in 1985.[28] Janet Morley offers a typically sparse and freighted version, followed by a series of prayers working through the petitions, in *All Desires Known*.[29] The St Hilda collection of services and prayers, *Women Included*, offers three versions of the Prayer of Jesus: Lala Winkley's version, one by Monica Furlong which begins 'God who cares for us', and yet another somewhat sparer version by Jim Cotter, 'Beloved, our Father and Mother', more appropriate for regular use (which comes originally from his *Healing – More or Less*).[30] I have found dozens of other versions online[31] and doubtless, new ones are continuing to proliferate. Recently, there has been a resurgence of interest in Aramaic versions of the Lord's Prayer, some of which are sung, presumably as a means of coming closer to the original language and thought-world of Jesus and his early disciples.[32]

* * *

---

28 In Hannah Ward, Jennifer Wild and Janet Morley (eds), *Celebrating Women: The New Edition* (London: SPCK, 1995), p. 43.

29 Janet Morley, *All Desires Known: New Edition* (London: SPCK, 3rd edn, 2005), pp. 119–24.

30 The St Hilda Community, *Women Included: A Book of Services and Prayers* (London: SPCK, 1991), p. 63; Jim Cotter, *Healing – More or Less* (Sheffield: Cairns, 1987), p. 51.

31 See, for example, www.elkgroveumc.org/wp-content/uploads/2017/05/Alternative-versions-of-the-Lord.pdf (accessed 23.08.2021) and https://rainbowcathedral.wordpress.com/prayers/ (accessed 23.08.2021).

32 See, for example, the Abwoon network, which seeks to make the Aramaic version of the Lord's Prayer widely known, used and learnt: https://abwoon.org/library/aramaic-prayer-meaning-and-movements/ (accessed 23.08.2021).

I found myself, over the course of some months in 2017, almost by accident, writing a sequence of prayers responding to and wrestling with the Lord's Prayer. I really can't remember now why or how I started, but perhaps it is not surprising that this prayer that has lived in me for decades, taking many forms and being part of much collective experimentation, has finally bubbled up into a self-conscious process of exploration. Like my earlier books on Mary and Christa, this one is a project of experimentation in which I have taken a core component of Christian theology and spirituality and subjected it to examination from many different angles and perspectives; but this time it is a text rather than a symbol that is the focus of the exploration or, as I prefer to name it here, improvisation. I am not so much attempting my own 'versions' of the prayer (though there are a few of them, and this chapter begins and ends with some), as riffing off the prayer in a wide range of ways, doing my own thing around the central words, images and themes of the original, rather as a jazz player might riff around a well-known tune. The original can be recognized, more or less (although in some jazz versions, the listener would be hard put to identify the tune if they were not told), but the jazz singer or player can take the original off in any number of directions and ways, stretching and experimenting with the given notes until they become their own thing.

'Improvisation' has been used as a metaphor by a number of theologians to describe the process of interpretation of biblical texts and, more significantly for our purposes, the processes of praying. Ash Cocksworth quotes with approval David F. Ford's work on improvisation, especially as applied to the ways in which the fourth Gospel takes up themes and symbols from the Synoptics and reworks them in original forms.[33] Thus, while John's Gospel does not contain many of the key incidents

---

33 David F. Ford, *The Drama of Living: Becoming Wise in the Spirit* (London: Canterbury Press, 2014) and *Christian Wisdom: Desiring God and Learning in Love* (Cambridge: Cambridge University Press, 2007), quoted in Cocksworth, *Prayer*, pp. 125ff.

or texts to be found in the Synoptics – no Lord's Prayer, for example, no institution of the Eucharist, no parables of the lost and found – nevertheless, themes and language from each of these are woven into the Johannine discourses in ways which suggest the writer knew the originals well and has meditated upon them at depth to produce fresh improvisations. Thus, for example, there may be no Lord's Prayer in John, but the so-called high priestly prayer of chapter 17 has Jesus praying to his Abba Father and meditating on the nature of their relationship and the way in which Jesus shares that relationship with his disciples, inviting them into the heart of the intimate father–son, parent–child, mother–daughter relationship. 'Improvisations,' Cocksworth suggests, 'by nature, do not repeat material in either content or form. Instead, they expand, reappropriate and reimagine themes in a new way. They are variations on the same theme while revealing something new. They are recognizably similar and recognizably different.'[34] He goes on to argue that 'the Lord's Prayer is a remarkably adaptable prayer', capable of 'endless local and denominational variations in form, language and indeed theology'.

There is not, and never has been, a standardized way of praying the Lord's Prayer. Like John, we are to go deeper, go beyond the text, make new connections, reread, improvise and challenge what comes before.[35]

I have taken Ash at his word and made this my rule of procedure for the prayers that follow. Few of them follow the shape or pattern of the original (some do). Most of them are conversations with a key theme, phrase or idea in the original – daily bread, for instance, or forgiveness of sins, or the will of God – taking up the theme and exploring it from different van-

---

34 Cocksworth, *Prayer*, p. 126.
35 Cocksworth, *Prayer*, pp. 128–9. In a written note to me, Ash wonders 'whether there is a pneumatology going on here (any reference to the Spirit famously absent from the wording of the Lord's Prayer), but maybe the prompting of the Spirit is to lead into new truth, new understanding, and new unfoldings of the Lord's Prayer – non-identical repetitions, so to speak'. This is a fascinating idea, and one I will readily subscribe to.

tage points. This has not been pursued in idle curiosity so much as in the urgent business of prayer and everyday life, seeking to cry out to the God of the world and the Church in an effort to bring the needs of the Church and the world before the face of God. And first and foremost, of course, these improvisations are prayed to the God of my life, emerging out of my own need, confusion, anger, suffering or rejoicing – working the daily bread of whatever befalls me, and those around me, into prayer, an offering to God.

The prayers that follow are not intended, in the most part, for public prayer, although a few of them might be suitable for congregational use. Rather, they are conversations, dialogues, laments, cries to the Father Mother, Abba Amma God of Jesus from my own life and context and situation. They almost all (not quite) begin with the address 'Abba Amma' or, in reversed order, 'Amma Abba', or one or other of these two parental forms. (Like any rule, this one has needed to be broken from time to time, for particular reasons, only thereby reinforcing the centrality of the Abba Amma address in the remainder of the prayers.) Jesus' address to his Father God in the intimate Aramaic form of 'Abba' was clearly precious to the earliest Christians, preserved and imitated by Paul in his letters and by those who came after. Although Jeremias' claim that Jesus' usage of the term was unique has since been refuted, it certainly seems to have been distinctive of Jesus' prayer practice. I have expanded Jesus' address of God as 'Abba' to include the feminine form of this Aramaic parental form, 'Imma' or, as I prefer, 'Amma', in the conviction that all that Jesus intended to convey in and through his address of God as Father now needs both paternal and maternal imagery to encompass the fullness of divine love and the full stretch of the divine–human relationship. I stand with those such as Sallie McFague who, without rejecting the masculine form of address to God, insist that the Christian patriarchal heritage has been so skewed by and to the male (and the ruling elite male, at that) that radical compensation is required to bring about wholeness and healing in Christian thought and practice.[36] McFague offers core models

---

36 For wider discussion of the use of 'Father' as an address for God,

of God as Mother, Lover and Friend,[37] and while this volume attends in particular to the parental metaphors of Abba and Amma, it does not ignore McFague's, and indeed multiple other, terms for God.

As McFague and others have argued, the Abba God envisaged and revealed by Jesus subverts rather than supports patriarchal and paternal notions of masculinity that 'Father' may suggest to many in our own time. Jesus' Abba God demands that all are regarded and treated as brother and sister within a radical egalitarian familial structure, the new 'family of God' that overturns the hierarchical power structure of many traditional so-called 'Christian' families. Paradoxically, then, in order to be faithful to the Abba God of Jesus and the family relationships inaugurated by him, contemporary theologians and pray-ers require other language and terms that relativize and radicalize ruling notions of fatherhood. We can only pray to God as Father in the spirit of Jesus if we subject that language to radical critique and improvisation. One of the reasons I adopt 'Abba' and 'Amma' as primary prayer terms is precisely that they are *not* equivalent to our own terms, 'Father' and 'Mother' (though I do, on occasion, use these terms – particularly when I am praying in dialogue and frequently in conflict with my own parental inheritance). Precisely because these are terms from another language, the ancient Aramaic language of Jesus, they do not carry the same baggage as our own terms 'mother', 'father', 'mummy' or 'daddy' – and this may be one

---

and gender and God-language more generally, see Ramshaw, *God Beyond Gender*, as well as *Under the Tree of Life: The Religion of a Feminist Christian* (New York: Continuum, 1998); Sallie McFague, *Metaphorical Theology* (London: SCM Press, 1978) and *Models of God: Theology for an Ecological, Nuclear Age* (London: SCM Press, 1987); Ruth C. Duck, *Gender and the Name of God: The Trinitarian Baptismal Formula* (New York: Pilgrim Press, 1991); Janet Martin Soskice, 'Can a Feminist call God "Father"?', in Teresa Elwes (ed.), *Women's Voices: Essays in Contemporary Feminist Theology* (London: Marshall Pickering, 1992), pp. 15–29; and Sarah Coakley's extended discussion in *God, Sexuality, and the Self: An Essay 'On the Trinity'* (Cambridge: Cambridge University Press, 2013), among an extensive literature.

37 McFague, *Models of God*.

reason why Aramaic versions of the Lord's Prayer are enjoying renewed popularity. They do not come with the same long and painful patriarchal history. Of course, I am not trying to claim that these terms are 'pure' or neutral; like all language, they are freighted and weighted with human history and use. Yet perhaps because they have had far less usage in family life and in our religious traditions, they may be capable of reinvention, of reinvesting with fresh meaning and association.

To pray to God as 'Abba' and 'Amma' is to pray in solidarity with Jesus and the earliest disciples whom he taught to pray to God in this manner. It is also to pray in continuity with the early desert tradition of the abbas and ammas who left the cities in protest at their corruption and sought remote wilderness places to live out lives of solitariness and asceticism, yet in community. The desert fathers and mothers laid the foundations for the monastic tradition which has sourced and fuelled Christian prayer for centuries and shaped public liturgical prayer profoundly. This tradition itself – the desert tradition and monasticism – is by no means unproblematic for a feminist, enshrining what can be experienced as dangerous and dualistic theologies of the body, sexuality and femininity itself. Yet I, like many, owe a huge amount to monasticism for the nourishment and nurturing of my own prayer life and discipleship. In praying to the 'Abba Amma' God of the desert fathers and mothers, I am wrestling with this inheritance as well as honouring and blessing it.

* * *

The book unfolds, after this introductory chapter, largely following the shape of the Lord's Prayer.[38] Chapter 1 focuses in particular on addressing God as 'Abba' and 'Amma', rooting this in my relationships to my own parents. It is hardly possible to pray the Lord's Prayer without drawing deeply on our own relationships with our parents, whether knowingly or not. If we are to relate deeply and freely to God as mother or father, Amma or Abba, we will probably have to wrestle deeply with

---

38 For further information on the origins and inspirations of specific poems, please see the Notes and Sources section at the end of the book.

the wounds and hurts, as well as the joys and privilege, of our own relationship to our very human mothers and fathers. For some of us, it may not be possible to claim the human language of motherhood or fatherhood in our relationship to the divine, so deeply wounded have we been by our earthly fathers and/or mothers. That is not a decision that any can make for another, but each disciple must make for themselves; and it may be a choice that can change over time, as old hurts and wounds are healed. To pray 'our Father' or 'our Mother *in heaven*' is precisely to recognize that our heavenly Abba and Amma is *not* the same as our earthly parents, and that it is in God alone that true and pure parenthood is to be found and in whom existing notions of fatherhood and motherhood are transfigured (an idea explored in the prayer given on page 113). Be that as it may, it will be clear that some of the prayers addressed to Abba or Amma in this chapter are addressed, first and foremost, to my own parents; only in working out my need, anger, fear – and indeed, profound appreciation – in my relationships to my own parents, can I also work out the relationship to God as my Abba Amma.

Chapter 2 acknowledges that parental terms alone are insufficient as a repertoire for prayer, however wide we may stretch them and experiment with them. The focus of this chapter is on the hallowing of God's name and what it can mean to 'name' God. It offers a range of playful and experimental namings of God to place alongside the familial names of father, mother, sister and brother which are familiar in Christian discourse. I hope that these prayers illustrate Brian Wren's conviction that it is necessary to 'bring many names'[39] to the prayer and worship of God.

Chapter 3 ranges widely around the theme of the kindom of God, offered as an alternative to the monarchical image of 'kingdom'. Although there is only a difference of one letter between 'kingdom' and 'kindom', that one letter makes all the

---

39 Brian Wren's hymn, 'Bring Many Names', appears in *What Language Shall I Borrow?* (London: SCM Press, 2012, 2nd edn), pp. 137–8, as well as in the hymn collection *Bring Many Names: 35 New Hymns By Brian Wren* (Carol Stream, IL: Hope Publishing Company, 1989), no 9.

difference! Introduced into feminist and womanist vocabulary by the Cuban theologian Ada María Isasi-Díaz,[40] 'kindom' has now become well established as an alternative to notions of territory, rule or realm which may be unhelpfully present in 'kingdom' language. Prayers in this chapter explore what it might mean for the will of God to be done 'on earth as it is in heaven', for the 'kindom of God' to be established in our world and our lives.

Chapter 4 works with the central theme of 'daily bread', drawing on biblical, Eucharistic and banquet imagery in a range of ways. Some of the poems and prayers here were written during the early period of lockdown, when yeast seemed to disappear off the shelves along with other staple foodstuffs, and households up and down the land seemed to be baking bread. This chapter roots prayer in the earth and the body, celebrating as well as mourning both the generosity and the devastation of the planet and seeking to articulate the cries of the earth for redemption.

Chapter 5 concerns the petition for forgiveness of debts and sins, wrestling with notions of forgiveness which may be unhelpful or even harmful, seeking to pray for release from debts in ways that have socio-political purchase, as well as acknowledging my own need for pardon and release and my own struggles to forgive.

Chapter 6 improvises around the final petition in the Lord's Prayer, the prayer to be delivered from evil and to be kept from temptation. These are prayers that wrestle with, and groan under, the burden of collective as well as individual trial, wreckage and devastation, seeking to discern the presence and salvation of God in the place of evil and destruction. What does it mean to pray to God from the centre of the whirlwind and to trust God in the place where it seems as if evil will conquer?

Two further chapters offer fresh perspectives on the Lord's Prayer as a whole. Chapter 7 is a series of prayers from the

40 Ada María Isasi-Díaz, 'Kin-dom of God: A Mujerista Proposal', in Benjamin Valentin (ed.), *In Our Own Voices: Latino/a Renditions of Theology* (Maryknoll, NY: Orbis Books, 2010), pp. 171–90.

desert tradition which take as their jumping-off point some saying or story from the desert abbas and ammas. These are truly 'found' or even 'stolen' prayers, which use the ancient words of the ammas and abbas to craft prayers which I hope are in the spirit of the Lord's Prayer – brief, concentrated and simple prayers with the whiff of the wilderness in their wings and an economy of scale that reflects the need to preserve energy in the hostile environment of the desert.

Chapter 8 affirms that it is not only humans who pray; the wild and tame creatures who live alongside humans can teach us a thing or two about prayer. These are playful yet serious improvisations as I imagined how the creatures might pray the Lord's Prayer in their own distinctive tongues. Starting with the cat's prayer (of course), the chapter moves on to prayers on the lips of bird, dog, sheep, donkey, river, sea and mountain.

Finally, Chapter 9 brings the collection to a close with a series of prayers that pray towards our ultimate horizon, that of our own deaths. Writing much of this book during the time of Covid when, as it happened, several immediate family members died (of non-Covid-related causes), my own death and that of those I care about has become more real to me, creeping several paces closer to my daily breath. Of course, none of us knows the hour of our death and Christians in our own time are unfamiliar with the ancient habit of meditating upon our death, yet Covid may be teaching us to walk with death more closely and consciously than many of us in the rich North have had to do for decades.

Every prayer we make, however inadequate, is an opening, an invitation, a summons to the divine and to our own best selves; a voting with our lips and our lives for wholeness and justice, the mercy and forgiveness which we know we desperately need if we are to give ourselves wholeheartedly to the good works to which we are called. Prayer creates a space within which what we pray for can become more of a reality – if only marginally – than it was before. I offer these prayers in the hope that they may create such a space in the lives of those who pray them with me and maybe even for me, as I pray for my readers, whoever and wherever they are.

The Lord's Prayer

After John Wesley[41]

Abba Amma:
all good, all loving, all blessing,
our creator, author of our being:

You raise us from the dust of the earth
and breathe into us the breath of life;
you withhold no good thing from the work of your hands.

Our preserver who, day by day, sustains the life you have given;
of whose continuing love we now and every moment
receive life and breath and all things:

Father and mother of our Lord Jesus Christ
and all who believe in him:
Mother and father of all families in heaven and earth:

May you be known by all intelligent beings!
May you be honoured, feared and loved.
May your everlasting kindom come,

May there be an end of misery and sin,
of infirmity and death,
that all may be consummated in bliss.

May we love to do your will as the angels do.
May it be our meat and drink,
our highest glory and joy.

---

41 See Wesley's sermon on the Lord's Prayer, which can be found
in Rose, *The Lord's Prayer*, pp. 38–47 and online in various places,
including https://livinghour.org/lords-prayer/sermon-by-john-wesley/
(accessed 27.08.2021).

Give us all that is needful for the body
and the life of the soul,
our common and sacramental bread.

Remove every hindrance that prevents us
from loving and serving you.
Freely and fully do we forgive those who have wronged us.

Do not let us be lured and enticed into temptation
and make a way for us to escape all evil.
All glory and honour and worship are yours. Amen.

I

Abba Amma

To repeat what was asserted in the Introduction: when we pray to God as 'father' or 'mother' – or, indeed, in terms of any human analogy (lover, beloved, friend and so on) – we cannot do so without drawing on the very human relationships, either consciously or, more likely, unconsciously, which have shaped our deepest convictions about, and experiences of, fatherhood and motherhood. In the first instance, then, praying to God as our heavenly mother or father is bound to bring into play, for good or for ill, our relationships to our human parents or, if we have for various reasons not experienced a direct relationship to our biological parents, to those who have stood in as surrogate parental figures for us. More broadly, we will have imbibed cultural norms of parenthood, perhaps drawn from a variety of different cultural settings; and of course, norms about both motherhood and fatherhood are much in flux in our own time. Even if our own mothers or fathers conformed to traditional norms of motherhood and fatherhood, we all know other people's who represent different kinds of parental care and probably other figures in our lives who offered us contrasting models of parenthood. So we are likely to have experienced a range of different patterns and norms, all of which will inform, either positively or negatively, our understanding of the motherhood and fatherhood of God.

In this chapter, I draw quite explicitly on my relationships with my own parents in the prayers that follow. In some cases, they are addressed first and foremost to my own mother or father, and I have written them as ways of engaging and wrestling with the inheritance I have received from them: a mixed heritage of profound love and care, on the one hand,

and painful woundedness and wounding, on the other. The ways in which I have experienced human motherhood and fatherhood have inevitably shaped the ways in which I relate to God as mother and father, and in the prayers that follow I have tried to bring this to consciousness and offer the full inheritance of these relationships – with their blessings and their wounds, their gifts and inadequacies – as part of my prayer. Some are angry, some are sorrowful, some are glad and grateful, and others partake of a range of emotions.

Of course, to name God 'Abba' or 'Amma' is not quite the same as calling God 'father' or 'mother', since we are unlikely to have called our own human parents 'Abba' or 'Amma' – even if, when we were learning to speak, we will have done something similar ('mama' and 'dada' are not so very far from 'Amma' and 'Abba', after all). One of the reasons I consider the address 'Abba Amma' or 'Amma Abba' to be a helpful one in prayer is that it both connects *and* separates us, *at one and the same time*, from the deep unconscious shaping of our relationships to our own parents. The heavenly Abba, the heavenly Amma, is both like and unlike our own earthly fathers and mothers, and there is a lot of space in that 'like and unlike' relation. This is how any metaphor or analogy works, of course, calling attention to what may be similar between two unlikely terms (in this case, parenthood and God); but equally, drawing on the frisson of what is *unlike*. A good metaphor or analogy bears this tension of 'like and unlike' within it and possesses the energy of that tension, which infuses it with the power to connect. To call God 'father' may be to employ a 'dead metaphor' – one that is so familiar that we no longer see or hear it as metaphor at all – whereas to name God 'mother' still has the shock and energy of novelty for many of us who have not been accustomed to naming God in female terms. To name God 'Abba' or 'Amma' or, as I do in many of these prayers, as 'Abba Amma' and 'Amma Abba', possesses both the frisson of the new and the rootedness in the familiarity of well-known terms for God. And because both terms – abba and amma – have deep roots in Scripture, in the prayer practice of Jesus and in the early desert tradition, these terms also partake of an ancient authority which makes them more than the idiosyncratic or personal preferences of one author.

It is highly unlikely that all readers will identify with all, or even many, of the prayers that follow; what I hope the prayers might do is encourage readers to reflect on their own personal inheritance of relationships with their parents, for good or for ill, and to draw the energy of these relationships into their prayer. When our relationship with God is infused with the reality of our human relationships – in all their muck, murk and ambivalence – it can take us to new depths of honesty, openness and vulnerability and thereby to a new capacity to receive the love of God whom we encounter within and beyond every human relationship.

Behold your child

Abba Amma, I cry to you
behold your child

Amma Abba, I cry to you
hold your child

Abba Amma, I cry to you
enfold your child

Amma Abba, I cry to you
clothe your child

Abba Amma, I cry to you
ensoul your child

Amma Abba, I cry to you
embolden your child

Abba Amma, I cry to you
make whole your child

Amma Abba, I cry to you
know your child

Abba Amma, I cry to you
own your child

Amma Abba, I cry to you
behold your child

Born from your womb

Amma,
born from your womb,

I gaze at you,
your image mirrored in me.

Of your beholding there is no end,
you hold my life in the hollow of your hand.

I return it to you
from where it is given back to me.

All that is yours in me
is released, set free,

shared with those you've given me
to love and forgive

and hurt and learn to love again
until, pardoned and freed,

we learn to let go our need
to be needed, noticed, applauded.

In your disregarded, unrewarded life,
poured out again and again, time without end,

we'll find our way home,
back to the origin and source of all we've become:

children of one mother,
sister of all, to each one your brother.

At your breast

Amma. Mmmm.
Mouth-shaped nuzzle
at your breast.

Amma. Ahhhh.
Sigh of contentment
in your arms.

Amma. Ommm.
The originating sound,
wound of the world.

Amma. Am.
Assertion of basic existence,
is-ness of each one.

Amma: source
of life, bliss,
truth, breath

from whom I come,
towards whom I daily move.

Amen. Amen.

A prayer towards my mother

Mother, I am of you
made of your clay and your longings

Mother, I am like you
I know whereof I am made

Mother, I feel your pain as my pain
My heart beats as your heart

Mother, I see myself in you
I fear you and resist you

Mother, I am becoming you
Give me the love and wisdom to accept it

A mother's love

After Julian of Norwich

Amma, mother
your love and service to your children
is the nearest, readiest and surest
and we may trust wholly
in your will, your work and your ways.

Amma, mother
your sweet gracious hands
are ever ready and diligent about us;
in all your work
you take the role of a kind carer.

Amma, mother
you understand and know your child;
as we grow, you change
your ways of mothering to match our needs
but your love remains constant.

Amma, mother
sometimes you suffer us to fall
or to be sick in various ways,
yet you keep our bodies and souls
so that we are never in peril.

Amma, mother
as a mother tenderly wraps
her child in drapes of love,
so your love embraces, enfolds and encloses us
in your heart, where we remain for ever.

And in this endless love
is our soul kept whole.

Prayer of a fifty-six-year-old woman

let me not turn into my mother
let the surfaces of my house be empty
let my underwear be durable and sensible
the size of my knickers on the line cause no embarrassment
and let there be silk and extravagance
but not so as to be ridiculous
let my clothes not exceed my wardrobe
let me not accumulate teapots
let my mind retain a modicum of elasticity
let my sentences have order: one subject, well chosen
let me eschew sub-clauses
let me know when to stop talking
and choose my friends wisely
let neither my legs nor my wits fail me
let me prepare for my own demise
set my papers in order
give things away
leave no skeletons in cupboards or nasty surprises in my will
    (let me make a will)
let me decide what to do with my 120 journals charting my
    life since 1976
let me be patient with my partner
and grant her a full measure of patience with my foibles and
    accretions
the manifold weaknesses of mind and body
that are turning me more and more into my mother
let me look at my mother in the mirror and judge her kindly

A prayer to Mother God

God our Mother, Source of all life,
compassionate and present,
protector of the poor and the marginalized:

Stand with the women and girls of Africa,
especially those infected with HIV and Aids
yet still caring for the sick and the dying,
working to keep families and communities together:

God our Mother
Stand with all who would otherwise fall.

Stand with the women and men of Palestine,
estranged from their land and homesteads,
separated by the wall from their neighbours and fields,
restrained, restricted and frustrated in their efforts to live
   ordinary lives:

God our Mother
Stand with all who would otherwise fall.

Stand with the women and men of Haiti
working to rebuild their devastated towns and villages,
trusting in you for the livelihoods they do not possess,
for the stability and hope in short supply:

God our Mother
Stand with all who would otherwise fall.

Stand with women and girls in China
emerging from centuries of oppression
to find their freedom and their contribution to a new society
yet still facing discrimination, abuse, victimization:

God our Mother
Stand with all who would otherwise fall.

Stand with the poorest communities hit hardest by Covid,
losing jobs, security and businesses, still waiting for a vaccine,
mourning the loved ones they cannot visit or even bury,
exhausted and hollowed out by the long months of lockdown:

God our Mother
Stand with all who would otherwise fall.

A creed to our Mother God

Mother God,
you are our source, our primal matrix,
the One in whom we live and move and have our being.
Long before we were born you knew us.
In your womb you cherished and chose us,
tenderly forming each of our limbs and organs.
You continue to labour over us,
embracing the travail of our birthing with joy,
so that we may be refashioned
for life and hope and freedom.
You feed us with your very body:
we are made one with you in a sacramental sharing.
You gaze on us with infinite compassion
and we see our own image mirrored in your face.

Nothing in all creation can separate us from your love.
Though you seem to push us away
and refuse our childlike clinging,
your absence is a release
into the greater powers of our being.
As a mother sends her child into the world,
yet never abandons it or ceases to care for it,
so you send us, empowered
with the knowledge of your love,
to be children of your compassion,
parents to all creation, co-birthing
with you justice and peace in your world,
labouring with your Spirit for truth and beauty
to be made manifest in all the earth.

leaving

abba, daddy
maybe it's time i grew up and left home

maybe it's time i stopped
trying to win your approval

maybe i don't need to
compete with my brothers

maybe it's ok
for me to be different

maybe i can make my own way in the world
far, far away from where you started

abba, daddy i'm leaving
it's taken a long time to forgive you

you didn't know how to father
a daughter like me

you didn't know how to give
your blessing to a life like mine

you didn't understand my choices
couldn't come with me to places

far beyond your ken
it's taken me a long time

to accept you for who you are
and where you'll never come

abba, daddy, i wish i could
prise open your old, cracked heart

too late, daddy, now
for that   or perhaps

not late enough
perhaps when death comes close,

you'll give up your grip
and let go into the freefall

of love   abba, daddy
may it be   so
                              amen

When did you ever say?

Father, when did you ever say to me
'This is my daughter, the beloved
In whom I am well pleased'?

Father, my father,
I would have committed myself into your hands,
but you had no use for my offering.

Would that you had argued with me,
pleading for what your love required of me,
but I was always the one with the words.

Father, forgive, that I have strayed from your Devon lanes,
that I have grown far beyond you,
that I remind you of my mother.

Father, my father,
I am yet a long way off, travelling towards you,
but you no longer look for my approach.

Father, I have longed for you
to rejoice at my homecoming
but you declined the invitation to the banquet.

All that is mine is yours,
even though you cannot accept it.

Dutiful daughter

Daddy, you decided decades ago
that your life was over

declared an end to travels
out of the country

long after it became obvious
all the traffic was going to be one-way.

You turned your face to the wall,
started counting the ailments

any one of which
might be fatal

yet twenty years later
you're still with us.

Every Sunday I make
my dutiful phone calls

conversation about the weather
the garden, trips to the doctor.

You like to track my achievements,
note my lectures and preaching.

I'm not supposed to mention
anything that might upset you.

Reversing the roles

Abba Amma, you are old,
bodies and organs hurting,
medication and supplementary supports increasing.

Any pretence you might once
have held for an interest in my life
is fast fading or already dead.

It's my time, now,
to care for you. And now
I discover how hard it is to do.

I'm too far away, too busy
or preoccupied to give myself up
to the attention you crave.

I might once have managed it
before my head got so full
of books and meetings and projects,

before my body began
its own insistent complaints
against the way I am punishing it:

migraine, fibromyalgia, arthritis,
chronic fatigue. Maybe I could have
managed it before I got so tired.

Amma Abba, you are old,
and I, growing older, refuse
the wisdom that might yet save us all.

As death approached

so much that had been painful   /   fell away
without a crash or fanfare   /   the dividing wall came down
without effort or intention   /   love came close

I remember your gentleness   /   from childhood
I touch again your tenderness   /   sat on my bed
comforting me   /   smoothing my hair

most of our words now redundant   /   not much to say
Are you well? / *Is Rosie okay?*
Yes, we're fine   /   nothing more you can give me

and so it ended   /
a still small space of quiet   /   father and child
embracing   /   forgiven

God our potter, maker

Based on Isaiah 64.6–11

Abba our father
Look upon us as we pray

Amma our mother
Do not turn away from us

Pater potter
You have shaped us like clay

Mater maker
You have fired us in the flames of love

Do not reject us
For we are all the work of your hands

No one calls on your name
Or strives to lay hold of you throughout the world

Yet we cry to you
Who belong to you, who are yours

Abba Amma
Father Mother
Potter Maker

Intercessions for a baptism, and the Feast of the Presentation

For the potential and the risk of each newborn life:
Gratitude and mercy

For all coming to the waters of baptism today and those
who present them:
Gratitude and mercy

For the joys and the wounds of parenting and for all who
nurture and support life:
Gratitude and mercy

For the glory of God in the faces of those who receive and
those who give care:
Gratitude and mercy

For the insight that is both burden and blessing:
Gratitude and mercy

For the vision that both reveals and strips bare:
Gratitude and mercy

For the longings and desires of all nations for freedom
and justice:
Gratitude and mercy

For the differences in which we delight and those with which
we struggle:
Gratitude and mercy

For the faith that responds with thankfulness and the faith
that responds with foreboding:
Gratitude and mercy

For the pain that wounds and that teaches us courage and
compassion:
Gratitude and mercy

For the deaths that have revealed to us terrible beauty and
fearful vulnerability:
Gratitude and mercy

For ourselves, as we seek to follow faithfully in the footsteps
of Anna and Simeon, of Mary and Joseph and Jesus:
Gratitude and mercy

Teach us, gracious God,
to be faithful in our loving and hopeful in our losing,
courageous in our actions and wise in our waiting,
honest in our perceiving and thankful for what we are
spared knowing,
that we may offer all that we are and long to become
to Jesus Christ, the one who was offered for us.
Amen.

2

Hallowed Be Your Name

The biblical and traditional invocation to call upon God as 'abba, amma', I want to insist (along with many others), must not be used to limit our praying and conceptualizing of God to these terms alone. If we *only* used biblical terms or metaphors for God in our speaking, singing and praying, we would hardly exhaust the enormous plenitude of what is available to us within the biblical texts and traditions. When Christians call upon their brothers and sisters to think or act or speak more 'biblically', I often want to say, 'Amen!' but go on to say, 'If you want to be biblical, be fully rather than selectively biblical.' I sometimes wonder what Bible some of my Christian brothers and sisters are reading, for it doesn't seem to be the same one that I am reading. Yes, by all means, let's call God 'father', but let's also use the full range of other parental imagery – God as mother bear, mother eagle, mother hen (many of these images of maternal love are shockingly fierce, even violent); and let's utilize the whole host of other human images and metaphors for God – God as lover, husband, betrothed, beloved, friend, stranger, trickster and enemy (among many others). And then, let's go beyond the human realm to call upon God as refuge, fortress, rainbow, storm, wind, flood, river and rock, fire, tempest and breath. And, if we should come to an end of praying in the terms and names offered us by our Bibles, let's then explore and exploit the immense riches of Christian and mystical tradition – itself inspired and nourished by the biblical witness, and a form of commentary upon that primary biblical testimony. And, if our lives should be long enough to exhaust these riches (and which could possibly be?), let's reach out further to traditions beyond our own: to the Jewish roots of Christian faith, and to contemporary forms of Jewish theology and belief, as well as to the wisdom and riches of other religious traditions.

'Bring many names', as Brian Wren's wonderful hymn puts it, and then goes on to offer new and old names for God: 'strong mother God', 'warm father God', 'old, aching God', 'young, growing God', developing each one in powerful ways. Being biblical, let's agree, is so much more than simply parroting the words of Scripture; it is to think and speak, to bless and pray, in terms as adventurous, daring, creative and startling as the biblical writers and thinkers themselves employ. We do them a disservice, as well as the God in whose name they write and speak, when we limit the mystery and glory of the divine to familiar forms and formulae. Being made in the image of God means at least that we are called to be as inventive and creative as the biblical God who is forever bringing new forms and life into being. Let's not bore God or each other with our own tired and timid terms, but revel in the freedom of speech and thought that might attract others to join our worship and prayer.

So in this chapter, I celebrate and advocate some of the many names of God which can stand alongside, and enter into playful dialogue with, the primary, familial names of Father, Mother, Sister, Brother, Abba, Amma, Daughter, Son, Parent, Child. As we hallow the whole range of biblical and traditional names for God, and as we mint new terms for the holy, so we may glimpse more and more of the holiness of our own human lives, and the beauty and holiness of the entire created order. This is very much in the spirit of an alternative petition in the Lord's Prayer which Ash Cocksworth alerts me to, alluded to by Gregory of Nyssa, in which the first petition was the so-called 'pneumatological petition', invoking the Holy Spirit in a sort of epiclesis, brooding over all prayer and language for God. As Gregory of Nyssa reports it, 'instead of "thy kingdom come" it reads "may thy Holy Spirit come upon us and purify us"'. As Ash comments, 'I like the idea of the Holy Spirit as the driver of improvisation, inspiring us to inhabit fully the abundance of God in our naming of God and in so doing transforming our language inside out.'

Hallowed be your name

Abba Amma
Hallowed be your name

Mother Father
Hallowed be your name

Sister Brother
Hallowed be your name

Grandmother Grandfather
Hallowed be your name

Lover Beloved
Hallowed be your name

Companion Stranger
Hallowed be your name

He, She, Zhe, They,
Hallowed be your name

Known Unknown
Hallowed be your name

Bird Bear Lion Lamb
Hallowed be your name

The Great I Am
Hallowed be your name

Rock Refuge Pillar Stone
Hallowed be your name

Cloud Fire Water Storm
Hallowed be your name

Spirit Comforter Strengthener Friend
Hallowed be your name

Thou Breath Heartbeat Pulse
Hallowed be your name

Nameless Silence Wonder Love
Hallowed
Hallowed
Hallowed be your name

Praying the alphabet

abba, amma
abbey, anchor
abiding
ablution
abolition
aboriginal
abounding
abridging
abroaching
absconding
absence
absolute absolution
absurd abundance
absorbing abyss
accessible acceptance
accommodating accident
accumulating accountant
accompanying accordion
ace, accuser, ache
acquittal, acrobat
acropolis
act, actor, action
actuality, acumen
addition
administrator
adventure
adversary
aeon of aeons
agape
ages of ages
agnus dei

agreement
aggrieved
aha! aid, air, aisle, alarm
alchemist, algebra
alibi, alien
all in all
alleluia, allogamy
allowance
alloy, ally
alpha, alphabet
altar, alternative
altitude, ambassador
amber, ambiguous ambit
ambrosia, ambulance
Amen.

God beyond binary

God between us
God within us
God against us

God alluring
God annealing
God overcoming

God in unity
God in trinity
God in multiplicity

God in translation
God in transposition
God in transition

God as noun
God as verb
God as preposition

God in centripetal pull
God in centrifugal push
God in spiralling motion

Hub, spokes, wheel
Circle, circumference, centre
Petal, stamen, stem

God, G-d, Godde
He, She, Zhe
Named, Nameless, Naming

Knowing, no-ing, no-thing

Our light and peace and joy

After Symeon the New Theologian

Abba Amma,
our light and peace and joy,
our life, our food and drink.
You are our clothing,
our royal robe,
the tent in which you deign
to dwell near us.
Our East and Easter,
our resurrection and repose,
our baptism, bath,
running river, source of life
and flowing stream.
You are our daily fire,
our bread and wine,
our banquet and every pleasure
we may please upon.
Sun without setting,
star always shining,
flame never consuming,
the lamp that burns within the soul's dwelling.

Jesus my brother

Jesus, you were the elder brother I never had.
You looked out for me, gave me wise counsel
when I asked for it and held back when I didn't.

You believed in me when I didn't believe in myself.
You saw my potential long before I did
and envisaged a bright future for me.

When I lost my way, you came after me.
You rescued me when I fell in dark places,
picked me up and carried me when I was bruised.

You watched me grow and, the more I grew,
the more you melted into the shadows,
letting me find my stride, make my own way in the world.

You stayed in the background in case I should need you
until I needed you no longer like that any more
and you disappeared completely and I knew only your absence

only to return years later in a different guise: as a sister,
a neighbour, a friend, as the brother who needed me
to lean on and to love him. Welcome back, brother.

Mother of the broken-hearted

O mother of the broken-hearted
have pity

Father of the crushed in spirit
have pity

Sister of the shamefaced
have pity

Brother of the bruised and faint
have pity

O grandmother of the little ones
have mercy

O grandfather of the comfortless
have mercy

O mother of mercies
gather into your arms the starving babies of the world

O father of compassion
let not one abandoned soul be left to cry alone

O sorrowing sister of the suffering
stand with all who weep

O brother of the broad shoulders and the brave heart
bear the burdens of all who are falling

O grandmother
O grandfather
O mother
O father
O sister
O brother

Hold and heal all that is broken, estranged and without hope
May your heart bear what cannot be borne
Nor crack under the strain

Amma Abba,
have pity

Name above all names

Abba Amma
Living One
Name above, within,
beneath all names
Great I Am
mysteriously indwelling
manifesting
in all that lives
in earth and seas
and heaven

Jesus Christa
fleshly Word
unheeded Wisdom
crucified king
reigning slave
bound liberator
uncontainable incarnate
abandoned lover
ever-loving pursuer

Holy Spirit
animating breath
germinating warmth
revivifying touch
testifying truth
convicting judge
generating hope
permeating life

Through all your names
new and old
forgotten, abandoned, undiscovered
yet to be

Behold!

we adore
we praise
we worship

Friend of the world

After Sallie McFague

Friend of the world,
of each atom, star, stone, fish,
baby, beetle, barnacle,

your love chooses
every particular thing about us
and cherishes it,

rejoices in what we are
and praises it to the rafters,
applauding us to become more.

In your friendship
we can lay our competition down,
give up all hierarchies.

We need not think ourselves better than
butterflies, bonsai, boulders
or worse than film stars, professors, bestseller novelists,

solar systems, galaxies.
All of us belong to each other and to you.
There's room for all at your party.

I come to you

Abba Amma
I come to you
no slave, but your heir

Abba Amma
I turn to you
no stranger, but a friend

Abba Amma
I cry to you
no subject, but your kin

Abba Amma
I pray to you
not out of fear, but in trust

Abba Amma
I run to you
expecting nothing, receiving everything

Abba Amma
I belong to you
your Spirit abiding in me, and I in you

Abba Amma
you pray in me
my wordless cries, your Spirit's sighs

Abba Amma
you live in me
my breath your breath, your life my own

Holy holy

Abba Amma
Holy holy

Father Mother
Holy holy

Sister Brother
Holy holy

Fire Water
Holy holy

Earth Heaven
Holy holy

Light Darkness
Holy holy

Spirit Body
Holy holy

Travelling Dwelling
Holy holy

Falling Gathering
Holy holy

Garden City
Holy holy

Word Silence
Holy holy

Time Eternity
Holy holy

God my clothing

After Julian of Norwich

God, my nakedness and my covering:
strip me of all that protects me
from self-knowing, genuine loving;
clothe me with the glory that is your likeness,
your incarnate Wisdom,
Jesus Christ.

3

Your Kindom Come, Your Will Be Done

The monarchical, hierarchical and patriarchal language of 'kingdom' is problematic for many of us who pray the Prayer of Jesus: not only feminists and those who object to imaging God as a powerful ruling male, but also republicans and all who believe in egalitarian styles of decision-making and leadership. It is what Gail Ramshaw describes as 'the myth of the crown', and to pray 'your kingdom come', without irony, qualification or subversion is to reinscribe unhelpful and unjust theologies of God and also to situate ourselves as citizens with little agency or power.

In fact, as many commentators point out, in Jesus' usage, to pray for *God*'s kingdom to come and to invite his followers to do likewise, was a radical political act potentially liable to punishment. Just as when the earliest disciples confessed 'Jesus is Lord' as a radical alternative to the lordship of the Roman Emperor, refusing thereby to honour the Emperor as divine, so to pray for God's kingdom to come *on earth* is to challenge and subvert the political reign of Rome. In effect, to pray 'your kingdom come, your will be done on earth as it is in heaven' is to say: the world belongs to God, and God's is the power and the authority, over and above every human realm, monarch, state leader or form of government. In contrast to the martial, stratified and repressive reign of Caesar, Jesus embodies a form of government that is vulnerable, peaceable, non-violent and radically counter-cultural. Paradoxically, then, just as to pray to God as the Abba-father of Jesus is to radically undercut patriarchal notions of fatherhood, so to pray for God's kingdom to come is to challenge and subvert ancient and contemporary notions of political, economic and social power.

Nevertheless, for many of us the language of kingship, kingdom and fatherhood has become so debased by centuries of patriarchal, kyriarchal and colonial usage that we cannot use these terms without severe difficulty. It is significant that, in the Gospels, Jesus is highly ambivalent about the language of kingship when applied to himself. 'You say that I am a king', he says in Luke 23.3 and John 18.37 when Pilate asks him, 'So you are a king?' Many of us are similarly ambivalent about the language of kingship, patriarchal rule and colonial power. We need new terms to signify new (old) meanings, at least to place alongside the old terms, if not to replace them altogether. There are alternatives or correctives to such imagery, developed by theologians and creative writers, which we may utilize in our thinking and praying. A subtle difference is made by praying for God's 'kindom' to come, rather than kingdom, for instance; as pointed out in the Introduction, 'kindom' is a term introduced to feminist theology by Ada María Isasi-Díaz, the Cuban 'mother of Mujerista theology', as she has been called. She herself learned it from a friend, a Franciscan nun named Georgine Wilson, and incorporated it into her own writing and thinking; it is now widely used by many who wish to avoid kingdom language. Although the linguistic change is a small one, it is a reminder of a much bigger conceptual and theological shift: from colonial conquest to the power of the oppressed, from the rule of the rich elite to the reign of the ordinary, uneducated poor, from the hegemony of male heteropatriarchy to the anarchic diversity of queer subversion. Stephen Cherry commends the usage of 'kindom' language when praying the Prayer of Jesus, emphasizing the importance of the notion of solidarity to Isasi-Díaz, 'the union of "kindred persons" who have a common interest and whose relationships are imbued with mutuality'. Cherry summarizes: 'Solidarity is the virtue of those who accept their interconnectedness and then respond to the oppression, pain and injustice experienced by others as if they were members of the same caring family.'

Other conceptual and symbolic alternatives to 'kingdom' imagery are offered by John Dominic Crossan, in his analysis of the Lord's Prayer. He suggests that a dominant image beneath and within the prayer is that of the 'household', with God imaged as the householder of the world, God's household or home. This literally homely image is one we may be able to relate to rather more readily than that of the kingdom, and has inspired several prayers in this book. Crossan relates this image of the household to the image of the sheepfold and Jesus as the shepherd – an image which has often been found problematic by modern urbanites, but for Crossan is an image of the kindom as a small farm where the farmer or shepherd cares for all the animals as well as the humans within the complex community of the farm. As one who was brought up on a small mixed farm of several households, paid workers and many animals, I resonate with this image to some degree. As anyone who comes from a farm knows, this is a far from romantic image. Farms are challenging, messy places where the business of caring for all within the remit of the farm goes on day in, day out, in all weathers. Small farms in particular (in contrast to massive agri-businesses) are often fragile economic units, frequently on the verge of crisis or collapse, and farmers are prey to depression, isolation and all manner of other challenges, financial, practical, social and psychological. Thinking of God's kindom as a small, well-run farm where the complex dynamics are managed for the well-being of all, may resonate more than images of a plush, well-run monarchy – which few of us have close experience of.

Whether we have much experience of farms (I recognize that the majority of contemporary urbanites will not), the notion of the household is one that all can relate to, is adaptable to a range of models of nuclear and extended families, and can speak of the kind of solidarity Isasi-Díaz's 'kindom' commends to those who pray the Prayer of Jesus.

God our affinity

Abba Amma
our affinity
our family
our only nationality

Amma Abba
our bearing
our bond
our belonging

Abba Amma
our care
our cherishing
our clothing

Amma Abba
our goodness
our forgiveness
our only frame of reference

Bone of your bone

Abba Amma
you have formed us in your image
you have made us in your kindness

bone of your bone
flesh of your flesh
we are your kith and your kin

we are one with you
knit to you
wed to you

your kindness is our bliss
your courtesy our home
your closeness our clothing

like a lover you woo us
like a mother you feed us
like a brother you guard us

in you we are never lost
from your love we are never cast out
in your family we always have a place

Amma Abba
our kindness   our goodness   our forgiveness
our kindom

The kindness of God

Amma Abba
your kindness is courteous
your nearness is gracious
your sweetness is luscious

you approach us so shyly
you woo us so tenderly
you beseech us so gravely

no kindness is too much for you
no tenderness too forgiving
no graciousness too forbearing

how can we know ourselves so blessed?
how do we find ourselves so loved?
how dare we hope ourselves so desired?

Ah, sweetness ineffable!
Kindness unspeakable!
Tenderness unbelievable!

On earth as it is in heaven

Amma Abba,
on earth as it is in heaven
may your kindom come

in the dirt of the ground
from whence all things grow
your kindom come

in the mud that we use
to build our homes
your kindom come

in the soil that we tend
to produce our food
your kindom come

in the compost of our hopes
and dreams, our common good
your kindom come

in the loam of our flesh
our bodies and blood
your kindom come

in the muck of our hate
the stench of our wars
your kindom come

in the fields of our dead
layered thick in the soil
your kindom come

in the clay of our lives
misshapen and reshaped
your kindom come

in the ash of what is
scattered, blown in the dust
your kindom come

in the clay, in the dust, in the ash
your will be done
your kindom come

on earth as it is in heaven
your kindom come

Your will be done

Amma Abba
your will be done

What does a father want for his children
except that they be well and happy,
live free of harm
and cause no harm to others?

Amma Abba
your will be done

What does a mother desire for her offspring?
Only that they flourish,
know they are loved,
bring joy into the world.

Amma Abba
your will be done

What does any parent want for their household?
That they live together peaceably,
learn to respect each other,
do not bring the family name into disrepute.

Amma Abba
your will be done

What does God desire for God's children?
Only that we act justly, love mercy and walk humbly
with our God all the days of our life.

Prayer of the household

Amma Abba
Householder of our world's hearth

Teach us to care for our planetary home
as we care for our own households

To provide for each one's need
and to share equitably what we have

To welcome the stranger
across our thresholds

To proffer water for dusty feet
and rest for weary souls

To treasure the manifold glory of creation
and to protect endangered species

To forgo the greed that sucks up oil from the depths
and razes forests to the ground

To regard the wreckage of our fragile earth
and to turn back from the harm we do

To show our respect for you
by the way we care for what speaks of you

In the shepherd's fold

Abba Amma
your kindom come
in the well-run home, the family farm

where fields are tended
animals fed and watered
buildings kept in good repair

where children and elders
are loved, clothed and sheltered
the sick and frail given special care

where all have a place
there is work for all to do
and shared reward at end of day's labour

where all gather round the table
receive food to satisfy hunger
and space to speak of what matters

where each sleeps peaceably at night
fearing no thief or intruder
trusting in the security of fence and wall

where human and beast may go in
and out and find good pasture
in the care of the shepherd's fold

To be holy and human

Abba Amma
it is from you
that we learn
how to be truly human

It is from the child
you sent as
the Human One
that we learn
how to live
as your children

Your Holy One
brought down
the kindom from on high
to establish it
in the lowliness
of our midst

to show us
how to live
in peace
on earth
as in heaven

So teach us
to become holy and human
in all that we do and say

Teach us to live
on the earth you have given us
as you live
in the heaven of heavens

a true community of love
a commonwealth of justice
an upside-down empire
where the child is crowned with the lamb

Parable of the mustard seed

The kindom of Christa is like
a bush that grows from a seed –

not very big, not grand
like the lofty cedar in danger of being toppled;

just big enough to provide shelter for many kinds of birds,
an eco-system supporting the life of
      robins, blackbirds, sparrows,
        beetles, spiders, caterpillars, ants.

Every year, it gets hacked back to the ground,
yet grows again from the seeds it produces,
recycling itself as love does, and life.

The descending way

Abba Amma
by your Spirit move us

from adoration to intercession
from worship to work
from abiding to doing
from the infinite to the finite
from the splendour of God to our distracted world
from joy of heaven to pain of earth

Take us on the descending way
to enter into the common life of the world,
there to accomplish your redeeming work.

And lift us up, at the last,
to sit with you in glory.

The threefold cord

Abba Amma,
whose will I do not know yet seek to do

into your infinite mercy I commend my way
into your everlasting love I abandon all that I am
into your mysterious purpose I commit my life

Take me as I am
Bless me for what I shall be
Break what still resists your work in me
Share whatever I have that may help to accomplish your will

Unite my will with yours
Plait the threefold cord of desire, intention and action
into a single cord of love that will not break

A prayer for our work

Amma Abba
>
> may we work with zest and care
> whether our work is burdensome or light
> whether it brings us pleasure or woe

Give us the grace
>
> to take on the job that needs doing
> the machine that needs tending
> the task that brings little reward or satisfaction
> the colleague who needs supporting
> the student who is draining and demanding

Give us the equal grace
>
> to relinquish the work we have relished when it is
>   taken away from us
> to lay down our work at day's end without reluctance
> to let much of what we do remain hidden and
>   unapplauded
> yet not to practise false humility

Teach us
>
> to judge and value our work rightly
> to do it as well as we may
> yet hold it as lightly as yesterday
> and allow it to fall away in the light of eternity

Looking towards the promised land

We've learnt to survive in the wilderness;
are we ready yet for the promised land?

We've filled our bellies hastily with the limited fare of
  sojourners;
are we ready to feast at our own tables on pomegranates,
  dates and figs?

We've worn thin our dusty pilgrim tunics;
are we ready to robe ourselves in fine silks and costly garments?

We've eked out an existence in alien territory;
are we ready to take possession of our own land?

We've been nomads, camping out in desert wastes, no place
  to call our own;
are we ready for a settled life, nowhere to escape to when
  things go wrong?

We've recited a history of slavery and shared oppression;
are we ready to make a new history shaped by responsibility
  and freedom?

We've railed against the power others have wielded over us;
are we ready to take up our own power, use it for each
  other's good?

We've stuck together in a hostile environment, sharing a
  common enemy;
are we ready to face difference and disagreement, the dialogue
  that comes with power?

We've kept each other going with the rhetoric of utopia;
are we ready to face the frustrations and disappointments of
  the real?

Intercessions for Easter Day

Jesus, we came to you at first light, with the women, clutching
    our spices,
but we found your grave disrupted and you were nowhere
    in sight.

Be with all who are perplexed and terrified this Easter day,
whose hearts are broken and faces bowed to the ground.

Give them the courage to open themselves to the terror
as well as the joy of your rising.

Jesus Christ, Christa:
in your rising, raise us.

Jesus, we remember your words of life and long to rise
    with you,
yet we are fearful to believe what we suppose to be an idle tale.

Be with all whose bold or timid voices are not heeded in
    our world,
and challenge those who prefer to give credence
to the narratives spun by wealth, privilege and status.

Give them the courage to open themselves to the scrutiny
    of truth.

Jesus Christ, Christa:
in your rising, raise us.

Jesus, in life you preached peace and went about doing good
   and healing;
yet many preferred violence and wilfully chose to destroy you.

Be with all who long for justice and do not have it,
and stir up those who have it within their power to bring
   about change.

Give them the courage and persistence to choose life
   over death,
peace over conflict, generosity over greed.

Jesus Christ, Christa:
in your rising, raise us.

Jesus, we think we know how your story ends,
yet your resurrection is not an ending but so many new
   beginnings.

Be with all who make the liminal passage of transformation,
and those who walk with them.

Give them the courage to embrace the risk of risen life
with both hands, without denying what went before.

Jesus Christ, Christa:
in your rising, raise us.

4

Give Us Today Our Daily Bread

The Prayer of Jesus falls obviously into two parts, each of three petitions. The first three petitions concern God, the hallowing of God's name, the coming of God's kindom and the doing of God's will on earth. Having established the primacy of God and God's ways and will, the prayer turns to the human realm and proceeds with three petitions: for daily bread, for forgiveness of debts and for deliverance from temptation and evil.

'Give us today our daily bread' is, perhaps, the simplest and most universal petition in the Lord's Prayer. Not a single earth creature can live without food, and 'bread' represents the staple foodstuff of very many cultures and countries – in all its huge variety, from the chapattis and naans of the Indian subcontinent to the ryebreads of Germany, the baguettes of France and the soda breads of Ireland. While this is a very real petition for daily food (not just bread – and we need to be aware that for those with coeliac disease or gluten intolerance, the image of bread may have its limitations), it represents far more than this. In a sense, this petition is a cry to the source of all life and sustenance for everything that is needful for our mortal life: bread and food, yes, but also water, the warmth and security of a hearth, the vital provisions of clothes and shoes to protect our bodies, a bed and somewhere safe to lay one's head, enough for our families and dependants, with some left over for the unexpected guest.

Enough for our daily needs, but no more. The prayer asks only that there is enough for today, *this* day; presupposing that the prayer will be repeated every day of our lives, binding the one who prays to faith and trust in God at the same time as building, day by day, that same faith and trust. To pray this prayer is to acknowledge our absolute dependence upon God for each day's provision, as well as our dependence on the earth of which we humans are the stewards. It is to remind us that God may indeed provide earth, seed, soil, sun and rain, but it is human labour that will bring in the harvest, mill the grain and turn the wheat into bread. It is, then, a prayer for our radical co-creatorship with God, as well as an acknowledgement of our absolute dependence. It reminds us of our vocation to tend the soil, to work the fields and to bring forth the bread we need to survive. It may also put us in mind of human creativity and imagination; while every human being needs daily bread (or its equivalent, such as rice or maize), the amazing variety and diversity of breads around the world, now largely available in supermarkets, as well as in cookery books and on websites for us to make for ourselves, teaches us that sustenance comes in many different forms and can be turned into something more than daily fuel.

At the same time, the petition for daily bread tutors the one who prays it into modest aspirations and gives no permission for hubris or greed. We are to pray only for what we need each day to survive and thrive; there is no warrant here for stockpiling or filling our barns with what we may need for the future. The prayer is in line with the parables of Jesus which teach the radical urgency of the kindom; the rich fool who pulls down his barns in order to build bigger ones will have his very life demanded of him (Luke 12.16–21), and of what use will his fortune be then? Those who follow Jesus in the radical dispossession of the gospel are admonished not to take on the journey more than they need (in Luke 9, the Twelve indeed are admonished not to take staff, bag, bread or money, but to be entirely dependent on the places where they will go, and the 70 sent out in Luke 10 are told to take no purse, no bag or sandals). The disciples are urged not to worry about their life, 'what you will eat, or about your body, what you will wear', for 'life is more than food, and the body more than clothing' (Luke 12.22–23). Rather, they are to 'strive for [God's] kindom', and all that they need 'will be given to [them] as well' (Luke 12.31).

This is a hard teaching for those of us who are rich, burdened as many of us are by the world's goods, with full barns, cupboards and groaning wardrobes. And not only weighed down by possessions, but by concerns and worries that distract us from the urgency and simplicity of the gospel. What can it mean for those of us who have not given up our possessions to live in poverty to pray this petition? At the very least, it compels us to acknowledge our own compromise with the world's ways and goods, and continually to lay bare all that we own and possess to the scrutiny of the Spirit. It does not mean that we should not take a proper and rightful responsibility for the future well-being of our own family or seek to provide for our old age. Whereas Jesus himself and his earliest disciples were expecting the imminent parousia, contemporary believers mostly are not, and we can hardly live in the world without concerning ourselves not only with our own future provision but, more urgently, with the future sustenance of our children and grandchildren on a planet which has a chance of surviving beyond the twenty-first century.

To pray this petition may help us to live more trustingly, more simply and sparingly, than we otherwise might do, and thus to do our modest bit to ensure the future well-being of the next generation and the survival of the planet: not to stockpile loo roll or yeast in a pandemic, to leave pasta on the shelf for the next person to feed their family, to consider whether we really need to take that holiday abroad and, if we do, whether we can travel by some other means than flying. It may help us to live more generously, and to share what we have with others. The prayer is not simply for 'my daily bread' but for '*our* daily bread', reminding us that we pray as part of a larger body of people, many of whom have far less than we do and may depend on us for the little they do have. At the very least, this prayer may help us to *want* to be more generous and trusting, even if we recognize that, often, we are grudging, grasping and fearful, preoccupied with our own immediate needs and wants or those of our immediate kith and kin. As Stephen Cherry points out, drawing on a sermon of Gregory of Nyssa, to pray for bread is to pray for justice:

For if God is justice, the [one] who procures [themselves] food through covetousness cannot have [their] bread from God ... For the bread of God is above all the fruit of justice, the ear of the corn of peace, pure and without any admixture of the seed of tares.

There is much more to the mystery of bread than these few brief comments can do justice to; not least, the mystery of the transformation of flour, yeast, salt and water through the combination of human labour (kneading) and warmth provided by God, offering a model of the transformation that is effected through the Eucharistic feeding that lies at the heart of Christian faith and worship. Augustine spoke of the Lord's Prayer itself as a sacrament, and so there is a kinship between this daily prayer and our regular feeding on the bread of heaven at the Lord's table.

Midnight prayer

Abba,
at midnight I come to you,
do not turn me from your door.

Give me three loaves:
for the unexpected friend,
for myself and my household.

Amma,
it is your child hungry for food.
Set some fish or egg in my dish.

Abba Amma,
you are the giver of all good gifts.
At midnight, in the noonday,
pour out your Spirit.

Our daily bread, broth, breath, breadth

Abba Amma, give us today our daily bread,
all that we need to keep body and soul:
sun and rain on our fields,
corn in our barns,
bairns in our arms,
a loving mate and friends,
peace in our land, good governance.

Give us today our daily broth,
the nourishing stuff that warms our bodies
and comforts our souls, the maternal soup,
the pottage that none can steal from us,
our parental birthright and blessing.

Give us today our daily breath,
clean, fresh air to fill our lungs,
and none to stand on our necks,
no poisonous fumes sickening our children to death.
Let us breathe freely and deeply,
that we may sing your praise truly.

Give us today our daily breadth,
the stature and scope to grow tall,
to take up all the room we were made for,
the wide-open space without bars
where our vision stretches as far as our dreams,
and both find their home, their hope, in you.

We are your children

Abba Amma,
we are your children
asking for what we need.
Do not give us a snake
when we ask for a fish!

Amma Abba,
we are your children
searching for the way.
Do not lead us astray
when we look to you for guidance.

Abba Amma,
we are your children
knocking at your door.
Do not send us away empty handed
when we come to you for bread.

Amma Abba,
we are your children
who know how to give
good gifts to our own.
How much more
can we expect you
to give us your Spirit
when we cry to you!

When we ask

Abba Amma,
when we ask
you will answer
though it may
take us by surprise.

Amma Abba,
when we seek
we will find
though it may not be
what we thought
we were looking for.

Abba Amma,
when we knock
the door will be opened
and you will be the other side
calling us into
a world we could never have imagined
where love rules over all.

The bread you give us

It doesn't belong to us.
It never did.
No one person possesses it.

The motley crowds that press
around you, exhausted and famished –

it's that raggle-taggle mob
who possess the answer
to their own clamouring.

We think we're running on empty.
We think we can't put another foot forward
without falling headlong.

Yet the very ones around us
begging for healing
give us the courage to go on.

Lying there barely able to breathe
or semi-conscious on their ventilators –

it is these, at the end
of all their resources,

who call out the springs of compassion
in others, fuel a determination to carry on.
The bread will not run out.

Prayer against worrying

Abba Amma,
you feed the ravens
and the wrens
which neither sow nor reap
and have no storehouse or barn

Teach us not to be anxious
nor to worry
knowing that life is more than food
and the body more than clothing

Amma Abba,
you clothe the lilies of the field
more gloriously than Solomon
or the Queen of Sheba
which neither toil nor spin
are alive today
and gone tomorrow

Teach us not to be anxious
nor to worry
knowing that life is more than food
and the body more than clothing

Abba Amma,
you have provided
grain and vines
enough to feed the world
and silks and cottons
sufficient to clothe us all

Teach us not to strive
for what we are to eat or drink
but to labour for your kindom
that all may be fed
and clothed and sheltered.

Let not our own peace
be bought at another's expense.

Gathering the fragments

Jesus, you do not turn us away
when we come to you
thirsty, empty, hungry,
desperately afraid.

You point us towards
resources in our lives
we did not even
know were there.

You take the fragments
we have gathered
and lift them up to become
so much more.

You bless our meagre supplies
and, even as you break them
into yet more morsels,
they are multiplied.

But only as we risk
giving them away
to the ravening crowds
urgently crying for bread.

You will not turn us away.
You insist that we, too, do not
turn away those whose cries
frighten and appal us.

The bread of tomorrow

Amma Abba,
give us today
the bread of tomorrow

the bread of sincerity
and truth

the bread of forgiveness
tough though it may be
to swallow

the bread of human dignity
that we receive
by putting it down

picking up the plate
of my own neediness

filled with fresh bread
by my sister, my brother

let me be fed
by others

so that I may learn
to receive

the gift of my being
the grace of your mercy

Abba Amma
feed me with this bread of heaven
the leaven of your kindom

Daily manna

Abba Amma: you have rained bread
from heaven for your people

You have given enough for each
no matter how much we gather

You have given us enough
so that we do not need to hoard

You have given us enough
so that we may share

You have given enough for each
so that none need ever go hungry

You have given enough
for each today and every tomorrow

You have provided double for the Sabbath
so that we may know we do not earn our daily bread

It is your abundant gift to us
overflowing in plenty to the day of resurrection

Yeast

Up and down the country
everyone is baking bread

adults forced to stay at home
teach children how to

mix the dough, get the temperature
of water just right

leave to prove, knead, then leave
again, in a warm place

for the damp mass to rise
double or treble in size.

It is what we are all doing
gathering what we find in cupboards

mixing it with salt tears, hopes, fears
saying our charms or prayers

for the ones we've lost
the ones we care for

those frontline workers
we'd love to sit down and feed.

We warm and work it
with our over-washed hands

then bake in the oven
smelling the fragrant offering

sweet as morning
breaking the loaf for others to eat.

The breads of the world

Amma Abba
give us today our daily bread

Let it be fresh
straight from the oven

Let there be dense wholemeal
thick with pumpkin seeds

Airy, light ciabatta
riddled with chewy holes

Fat yellow and yeasty buns
fragranced with cinnamon

Huge naan breads
hot and sweet from the pan

Roti, cooked
on the noisy streets of Kolkata

Slim baguettes
dipped into strong Parisian coffee

Dark, heavy pumpernickel
laced with rye

The ordinary bread of
every country and culture under heaven

brought to the banquet of the nations
where each may share the glories of their cuisine

Let us try all the breads
and admire each for their particular qualities

And let there be enough
to feed each one's hunger

and more than enough to spare

No yeast

So there's no yeast.
Make it unleavened, then,

as our long-ago ancestors did
in Egypt, in their hurry to be gone.

We long for release
from this imprisonment

as the numbers of dead grow daily
and fear stalks the corridors.

Yet there's no hurrying
this rising. It will take

as long as it takes, until
the ten plagues are over

and a nation of cherished
sons and daughters
                          slain.

Making soda bread in the blue kitchen

stirs memories of Evelyn serving it warm
from the oven in her Wimbledon home.

Most of the detail has flown but I remember
the way she was, her love of subtle shades of colour,

her delight in sharing food, her gentle laugh
and flash of wit in limpid eyes, the way she wove

love and light into the simplest offerings – a pot of flowers,
an afternoon's walk, years later, along a stony Cornish beach.

The loaf is rising in our Stirchley oven
while her cold body will soon be fired

to become God's bread; but oh,
that woven cloth of light and love

will flame out, like shining from shook foil,
over and over, a glory never to be done.

Give us this day our daily bread

Fruit that is grown
and eaten in due season
grains and pulses
that have not cost the earth

Strawberries, raspberries,
peaches and plums
we have waited the long winter for
like old friends or new lovers

Vegetables planted
with our own hands
on our little patch of soil
or bought from local farmers

Imperfect, oddly shaped,
dented and eaten splashed
with a little mud
yet tasting like heaven

Fish and seafood from waters
that are clean and will be replenished
Poultry and meat
that have ranged freely

None of it coated in plastic
or lavishly packaged
but wrapped in paper, cardboard
or a bag we have provided

Abba Amma
make us mindful
of the bodies we feed on
and willing to take
only what we need
that others may have
and eat their daily bread

Prayers for harvest (1)

Life-giving God, we celebrate your gifts of sun and rain,
blossom and bud, grape and grain. Give us grateful hearts
that overflow in praise. May all who plant and reap be
rewarded with a share in the harvest.

God of the harvest,
hear us.

Generous God, you send your sun to shine on the righteous
and the unrighteous, the deserving and the undeserving alike.
May those who have much be ready to share it, and those
who have little not be ashamed to receive.

God of the harvest,
hear us.

Sustaining God, we pray for the well-being of the earth
and for all who work to preserve and protect its fragile
ecodiversity. May the leaders of the nations commit to the
repair of the world.

God of the harvest,
hear us.

Protecting God, we pray for the cities of the world: for the
preservation of open spaces, of green growing things and
running water where birds and insects may find a habitat and
where human creatures may rest and play.

God of the harvest,
hear us.

Compassionate God, we pray for all who suffer want in the
midst of great plenty: for the hungry and homeless, those
driven from their lands by war or disaster; for any in pain
who cannot enjoy the good things of life. We remember
particularly before you ...

God of the harvest,
hear us.

Gathering God, we pray for all who have died, that their lives
may continue to bear fruit in those who mourn and remember
them, and that they may reap the joyful harvest of heaven.
We pray for ...

God of the harvest,
hear us.

Redeeming God, we pray for ourselves, that we may trust
your bounty in every season of our lives. Show us how to
trust in your word that never falls to the ground fruitless, that
always bears seed for sowing, eating and sharing. Teach us to
live as if 'all in the end is harvest'.

God of the harvest,
hear us.

Prayers for harvest (2)

For the grace of living
For the sweat of labouring
For the joy of harvesting
    Thanks be to God!

May those who sow in tears
Reap with shouts of joy.

We pray for all who work the land and harvest the crops: for
immigrant workers often labouring in appalling conditions
for pitiful pay; for farmers and fisherfolk working to make
a living against the odds; for those who labour for better
conditions for workers.

May those who sow in tears
Reap with shouts of joy.

We pray for places in the world where the land has been
devastated by war, drought, floods or other disaster: for
Darfur, Iraq, Israel and Palestine and other countries we
name in our own hearts.

May those who sow in tears
Reap with shouts of joy.

We pray for the leaders of faith communities: that they may
lead us in the ways of justice, peace and truth, that the hearts
of faithful people everywhere may be turned towards the
service of our neighbour and to the well-being of the earth.

May those who sow in tears
Reap with shouts of joy.

We give thanks for each person in this gathering, reflecting, in myriad ways, the glory and beauty of God.

Our seeds we bring, O God, that you may bless them.
Our hoes we bring, O God, that you may bless them.
Our hands we bring, O God, that you may bless them.
Ourselves we bring, O God, that you may bless us.

May those who sow in tears
Reap with shouts of joy.

We pray for all whose lives have been gathered up into the mysterious harvest of death, that the fruits of their lives may be a rich blessing for those who now mourn their passing. Especially we pray for ...

May those who sow in tears
Reap with shouts of joy.

Every day

Abba Amma
Every day teach me to pray afresh
and, if I cannot pray freshly,
receive the paltry offering
of my distracted repetitions.

Every day, I pray to you
for forgiveness,
daily bread,
protection from evil.

Every day, I will hallow
your sacred name.

Come rain, come sun,
come wind, come weather,
I will do it again.

In sickness and in health,
for better or for worse,
as I age and make my way
towards death.

Every day
I will begin again.

Prayer of the commode

After Kathleen Norris

every morning
emptying the stinking pot
down the drain

cleaning with running water
the vessel that will
receive human waste

giving thanks
for the functioning bowels
the body's dregs

receiving with gratitude
the comedy of grace

5

Forgive Us, As We Forgive

Forgiveness is at the heart of Christian teaching, and prayer for forgiveness lies at the heart of the Prayer of Jesus. Having prayed to God, the source of all material provision, for our daily bread, we next throw ourselves on the mercy of God, source of all love, healing and redemption, for forgiveness of our sins, even as we pray for the greater mercy required to forgive those who have harmed us or sinned against us.

To pray for forgiveness presupposes an acknowledgement of sin or failure, and this takes us to core Christian teaching about the fallen human condition, the way in which our humanity and the whole created order is marred by sin, the collective human need for forgiveness, restitution and redemption. Yet theologies of sin and forgiveness are fraught with difficulties, especially for women and for other groups which have been marginalized and othered by dominant Christian tradition: Black and Asian persons, sexual minorities, those differently abled, children and so on. Women have frequently been more sinned against than sinning, and there is a persistent tradition in Christian theology that holds women, in the person of Eve, to be responsible for bringing sin into the world and therefore more culpable than men, or Adam. Feminist theology has exposed this misogynist teaching, cataloguing some of its most horrific manifestations in the writings of the early Church Fathers and later theologians. Taking seriously the experience of survivors of physical and sexual abuse, a number of theologians have also challenged the unthinking and potentially abusive demand for those who have been abused (frequently women and children) to 'forgive' their abusers, to stay in violent marriages and to 'redeem' the violent partner or parent through their self-sacrifice and suffering.

More subtly, many modern accounts of sin have tended to reflect dominant notions of sin as pride, aggression, hubris and over-extension of the self, which may be far more likely to characterize the besetting sins of those with much power – white, heterosexual, financially secure men, for example. Valerie Saiving's classic 1960 essay suggested that the sins of women might take a different form, manifesting in a lack of self-worth and esteem, an underdevelopment of the self and a failure to claim one's agency and power. Western Christian traditions, particularly in their Protestant forms, have tended to focus on individual sin, repentance and conversion, rather than addressing the larger systemic sins which characterize society and our world, within which individuals' lives are meshed. The Seven Deadly Sins, popular in the medieval period, exemplify well this privatization of sin, and reflect, too, an unhealthy distrust and fear of the body. The sins castigated and abhorred in the list of the seven are no more than corruptions or excesses of entirely healthy human hungers: greed being rooted in a natural love of food, lust being a corruption of normal sexual appetite and sloth no more than the underside of the right and proper need for rest and sleep (and much the same could be said for the remaining four).

Thus, we need much discernment and discrimination in praying for, and with the notion of, forgiveness. The language of forgiveness needs to be used sparingly and attentively to the context and times in which it is used. Currently, for example, besetting systemic sins would include racism, ageism, the destruction of animal and plant species and the havoc humans are wreaking on the very cosmos which endangers all life. These are the blatant and most dangerous sins for which collective repentance is required, which jostle with the much more mundane and personal failings and foibles of individuals – so in what follows there is a mixture of confessions of a woman struggling to reduce what is in her wardrobe, to love her aging parents and be kind(er) to her own frail flesh, as well as to forgive someone who has caused her great pain, and to engage with the larger injustices of which she is a part. The larger and smaller sins, the individual and the corporate, are often profoundly connected: our struggles to resist a consumerist, possessive stance in our personal lives, in terms of what we buy or resist buying, are part and parcel of our collective endeavours to live more simply and sparingly in the world in order that other species may live and thrive.

The ways in which forgiveness has been imaged as a wiping clean of the slate, a divine forgetting of all that has been done, may not be the most helpful ways of thinking about forgiveness in systemic terms. Both receiving and genuinely offering forgiveness are rarely momentary acts, but usually lengthy processes marked by struggle, anguish and heart searching. Any theological or moral description of forgiveness that suggests that humanity can simply walk away from our collective responsibility to care for each other, the poor and the planet in which we live, will not serve. At the same time, the Christian gospel betrays itself if it ceases to preach the generous, merciful, overflowing divine love that makes the world and every creature in it, and loves each creature to the uttermost, endlessly giving of the divine life in the most costly ways imaginable in order to mend and restore what becomes broken and marred through human failure and sin. This profound truth, exemplified in the life and death of Jesus, has immense power to transform both individuals and communities, freeing human energies and ingenuity to be put to the service of the common good. Without forgiveness, those energies and prodigious talents are very likely to become centred on the self and the little world in which the self is enclosed, or to become perverted into deadly corruptions of the good and beautiful qualities they are. Unchecked, human power, wisdom and love can become corrupted into forces of domination, deadly destruction and the privileging of one group above another, with all the consequent terror and harm that can ensue. We certainly cannot do without the language of sin and forgiveness, and our need to pray daily for forgiveness is no less urgent than our need to pray for daily bread.

Confession

Abba Amma
whose world is not ours to possess
forgive us when we grab and grasp

Amma Abba
whose treasure is not ours to exploit
forgive us when we quarry and plunder

Abba Amma
whose territories are not ours to rule
forgive us when we conquer and invade

Amma Abba
whose generosity is not ours to query
forgive us when we limit and constrain

Abba Amma
whose compassion is not ours to question
forgive us when we criticize and condemn

Amma Abba
whose wisdom is not ours to marshal
forgive us when we assume to declaim

Abba Amma
all things are yours
and we only live on this earth out of your goodness

Forgive us

Not as we forgive others, God help us,
for often we don't. Or, if we do,
only grudgingly, eking it out
like the last spoonful in the last jar
of last year's jam.

As we would want to forgive others,
perhaps? But often I don't.
I want to hug my grievance to myself,
cherish the hurt I surely did not deserve,
relish that righteous feeling of being
badly treated, swelling with the indignity of it.

Forgive us, God, as only you forgive:
freely, without price or condition.
As – though we shudder to imagine it –
Christ forgave on the cross with his last breath.

When you forgive us like that,
what might it do to us but remake
our poor little self-absorbed hearts,
render us capable of the pity
on others you shower upon us

long before we ask for it,
long before we've even turned in our tracks
to face you, grasp the compassionate
hurt of you writ large on your
shockingly unprotected face,
see the tremor in your hands that long
to grasp our returning flesh?

Prayer for the imperfect work of parenting

Abba Amma, you are perfect parenthood,
the source and end of all true fatherhood and motherhood,
and we may trust wholly in your love.

Yet our parents bore us and nurtured us imperfectly,
bestowing upon us the pains and wounds of human relating.

Where they have hurt us, give us compassion
and understanding, that we may forgive.

Where they have abused us, give us the freedom
and wholeness for which we long, that we may be released.

Where they gave us a good enough grounding,
give us gratitude and generosity to accept what they could
    not give.

Amma Abba, in our own parenting,
may we love without wounding or,
when we wound, help us to tend the wounds.

May we love without abusing or,
should we abuse, help us to repair the damage.

May we love without pretence or the desire to possess
and, when our love falls short – as it surely will –
may our children have the grace to forgive us.

Confession for one who is rich

Abba Amma,
I live in one of the richest
countries in the world
yet over 14 million people
live in poverty in the UK

have mercy

Amma Abba,
I can walk to the shops freely
and buy whatever I like
yet thousands must procure vouchers
to get their basics from foodbanks

have mercy

Abba Amma,
I can cook anything I want
for my supper
yet millions of parents struggle
to put food on the table for their children

have mercy

Amma Abba,
I don't have to explain or justify to anyone
what I buy or cook or eat
yet those seeking welfare assistance
must lay their lives and financial struggles
on the line for others to scrutinize and assess

have mercy

Abba Amma,
making my daily bread
brings me only delight
while many who are hungry
know also the stigma of shame
that makes their bread taste sour

have mercy

A litany for Black Lives Matter

When did we see you, Lord?

When our sin stares us in the face
When we refuse to talk about race

When being black is a crime
time after time after time

When ethnicity
is a penalty

When I don't recognize
how privilege terrorizes

When I refuse to see
my own complicity

When a nation's wealth
is built on violence and stealth

When black bodies are still enslaved
and we feel no rage

When simply being black
is sufficient cause for attack

When it's unsafe to walk the street
because of the injury you might meet

When police do not protect
but target the very lives under threat

When we have to be told that Black Lives Matter
because so many have been shattered

When racism is not repented
and new forms of denial invented

When white privilege masquerades as the norm
and our leaders refuse to name and shame the harm

When we do not even see the sin
so cannot let forgiveness in

Confession of a middle-aged woman

Abba Amma
forgive my sins
of omission and commission

That my 'to do' list is too long
my expectations of myself
and others ludicrously unrealistic

That my wardrobe and cupboards
are stuffed with clothes I don't need
and cannot give away

That I can't stop purchasing
books I'll never now
get around to reading

That I can't seem to get around
to clearing the piles of files
in home and work studies

That, consequently, I never
have enough time
for my father and mother

That, day after day,
I am punishing my body
sitting too long at my desk

That I do not walk or swim
or even read the daily poem
I recommend to others

That I'm too distracted
to do more than listen to a summary
of the day's news as I fall into bed

That I barely read the newsletters,
appeals and magazines
that pour in from charities

That I promise myself
I'll find time in retirement
to work with the homeless, or refugees

I'll listen better to my mother
and visit my parents more
before they die

Confession for gender justice

Based on Mark 16.9–end

Forgive us, holy God, genderful and strong:
lead us into the freedom of being man, woman, other;
lead us into the freedom of being fully human.

We pray for a church that is open to newness,
ready to receive good news about the leadership of women
new forms of expressing the masculine
and ways of being human that go beyond the gender binary.

Forgive us, holy God, genderful and strong:
lead us into the freedom of being man, woman, other;
lead us into the freedom of being fully human.

We pray for a church that is open
to the manifold forms in which the Risen One appears,
ready to receive new wisdom from scholarship and experience,
as well as new readings of the Scriptures.

Forgive us, holy God, genderful and strong:
lead us into the freedom of being man, woman, other;
lead us into the freedom of being fully human.

We pray for a church that is open to being upbraided
for its lack of faith and stubbornness,
ready to believe others who have seen the Risen One,
and to embrace what may seem strange, unsettling, queer:

Forgive us, holy God, genderful and strong:
lead us into the freedom of being man, woman, other;
lead us into the freedom of being fully human.

We pray for a church that manifests the signs of God's
    new age:
that resists evil and stands against injustice,
that heals the sick and is not fearful to handle deadly things,
that risks its own life for the well-being of the world.

Forgive us, holy God, genderful and strong:
lead us into the freedom of being man, woman, other;
lead us into the freedom of being fully human.

How to forgive

1 It's going to take a long time. For a long time, you won't be able to do it.
2 The very thought of forgiveness makes you sick. Who says forgiveness is such a great idea anyway?
3 There's the shock of it, the numbness, the not-being-able-to-take-it-in, this attack you didn't see coming in a hundred years. How could you? There wasn't an inkling.
4 A well-meaning friend tells you to pray for your enemy every day for 40 days; then God will take the hurt away. You want to spit in his face.
5 You'll come soon enough to grief, howling at the moon for the precious thing that is broken, never to be repaired. Tears coat your every prayer.
6 Grief gives way to blistering rage, the anger of the jilted lover. You want to tear up all the books on forgiveness. You want to bring down hot coals on your enemy's head. You dream about smearing shit all over her desk.
7 Rage gives way to bargaining. You go over it, again and again, in your head. You try to work out how and why it happened. You talk to your silent enemy who will not talk to you, screaming at her and demanding an explanation. You try to find a way to fix it, right the irreversible wrongs. It plays and replays like a stuck record in your head.
8 All this time, there's no chance of forgiveness. Your mind and heart aren't ready.
9 Life moves on. You wake, you sleep, you eat, you wash your face, you go to work, you carry on all the old things that have lost their meaning and become mechanical. You smile, you speak, you walk around with the dagger stuck in your back.
10 At first, just for minutes and then for hours at a time, you catch yourself not thinking of it any more. Someone casually mentions your enemy's name and you do not flinch. There comes a day when no thought of her crosses your mind, no anger or grief or pity stir your heart.

11 One morning you wake with a start and find yourself thinking of your enemy without rancour. It's her birthday. You only wish her well.

12 Learning to forgive is not anything you do or deserve or understand or achieve. It comes to you one morning out of nowhere, when you know you are released. Your heart has been repaired and you have no more need of your old hurt. You can let it go. Your enemy departs with it, down the road and out of your life for ever.

A confession for returning

Mother, we have forgotten the old ways
Bring us back

Father, we have bypassed the untrodden routes
Lure us to them

Sister, we have erased the memory of the westerly skies
The lingering light on the sea

Brother, your wind-chafing voice
Has long since ceased ringing in our ears

As I walk these lonely sheep-strewn paths
and test my body's strength

As I empty my mind
of what I once regarded important

Remind me of who I am
teach me from where I have come

Show me the path I must walk on
tender to me the name by which I am called

The sins that cling

Abba Amma: release us all
from every snare
and thrall

Unbind our eyes
that we may see
the way to be free

Loosen the chains
that injustice may
no longer reign

Undo the wrongs we do
that we may know
we belong to you

May we live
in the wide-open space
your Spirit gives

that we may lift our faces
unashamed to your gaze
and receive your unending grace

to go on once again
released, set free
in the liberty for which we were made

and which we claim
in the name of your Son
the loving, freeing, releasing One

Confession for a lack of trust

When I fail to trust you and the frail human ones
who are your presence here and now in my midst

Abba Amma, forgive

When I cannot reach out to the hurting, frightened one
who needs my reassurance and hope

Abba Amma, forgive

When the hope shrivels up inside
and I succumb to fear and despair

Abba Amma, forgive

When I allow anxiety to cloud my vision of the future
and prevent me from taking risks

Abba Amma, forgive

When I speak harshly and without thought
and take pleasure in cutting the other down

Abba Amma, forgive

When I neglect my own inner, hurting child
who needs me to cherish and comfort her

Abba Amma, forgive

Confession for a lack of passion

When I do not trust my own deep hungers,
when I'm too scared to dream,
when I hold myself back from wanting too much,
telling myself, 'Don't be selfish! Don't be greedy!'

Or when I say, 'You won't get it! You don't deserve it!'
'Who do you think you are?'
'What gives you the right to hanker
after a life that can never be yours?'

'There are millions starving in Africa
while you're eating caviar and drinking champagne
and still wanting more?'
'Bad girl! Greedy girl! Impossible dreamer!'

When all the voices clamour
to drown out the lure to freedom,
to dampen the impulse to dream,
to limit the largesse of mind and heart –

Come then, liberating Spirit,
come with your lightning and scorch the dead wood that
    blocks out new growth;
come in torrential rain and soak the ground starved
    of moisture,
come with summer warmth to swell the hard grains
until they break open and put down roots,
send up shoots reaching for light.

Come to the tight, sealed, scared place of lockdown,
and break the bonds that imprison desire.

Receiving forgiveness

Expecting the barred gate,
we find it flung open.
'Come in, come in!'

Deserving or desiring punishment,
we are stunned to hear the charge:
'A total and non-negotiable pardon'.

Bowed down under the weight of sin,
we feel every burden lifted, one by one.
'Go free, go free.'

Knowing only shame,
we cannot believe love can look on us.
'How beautiful you are, my love, how lovely!'

Fearing to enter the banquet hall,
the host rushes out, ushers us in,
'Sit down, sit down!'

Our every penny spent, fortune squandered,
forgiveness makes us rich in what we had lost.
'Love paid the price, love sealed the bond.'

All purpose confused, every aim undone.
Alone, alone in the terrible wood.
One waits for us there, enfolds us in love.

'You were never lost in my love.
Welcome home, welcome home.'

6

Lead Us Not Into Temptation, But Deliver Us From Evil

Having prayed for all that we need for our sustenance, and for forgiveness, we pray now for protection against temptation and evil (or the Evil One, as the Greek text suggests). The Prayer of Jesus is realistic about our lives, that they are set in the midst of danger and evil: both physical danger and catastrophe, as well as moral, political and spiritual perils and dangers. This would hardly have needed to be highlighted for the first followers of Jesus, members of a colonized country under the imperial rule of Rome, subject to crippling taxes and violent coercion if they put a foot out of step. Public crucifixions – involving sexual as well as every other kind of assault and humiliation – were frequent reminders of the harsh penalty enacted on any who attempted to rise up against Roman rule. In 4 BCE, close to the time of Jesus' birth, Herod the Great died and revolts broke out all over the Jewish homeland. These were ruthlessly quashed and whole towns razed to the ground and their inhabitants taken as slaves. This would have been the obvious background to the prayer that Jesus taught his disciples, and thus John Dominic Crossan interprets this petition concerning temptation and evil as a quite specific reference to the political context. While there are many different kinds of temptation – moral, religious, political, economic – Crossan suggests that what is in mind here is the temptation to take up arms and resist Roman rule with violence, as many rebels did at the time of Jesus. Some of Jesus' followers may well have favoured armed revolt: Simon the Zealot, for example, was clearly a member of the group which advocated armed resistance to Roman rule. Yet Jesus' way was a way of non-violence, as we see throughout the Gospels, and he thus instructs his disciples to pray against the temptation to take to violence as a strategy against Roman occupation and oppression.

Both Luke's and Matthew's Gospels give us narratives describing the temptations of Jesus in the wilderness, marking the beginning of his ministry. The three temptations are to use miraculous power for personal use (to turn stones into bread), to make a public display of miraculous power (to cast himself down from the Temple) and to worship the tempter in order to win the kingdoms of the world. Crossan summarizes the opposing ways open to Jesus starkly: 'To obtain and possess the kingdoms of the world, with their power and glory, by violent injustice is to worship Satan. To obtain and possess the kingdom, the power, and the glory by nonviolent justice is to worship God.' Although the Gospels suggest that Jesus won a decisive victory over the tempter at this point, it is clear that the struggle against the temptation to accede to Satan's ways did not leave him. In particular, Jesus wrestles in prayer in Gethsemane, desiring that God will remove the cup of suffering from him.

Whether or not Crossan is right in his interpretation of this petition, to pray the Lord's Prayer is to sharpen our awareness of the choices we are daily confronted with, in our own times and world, *for* goodness and mercy and the reign of God and *against* the temptation to violence, evil and the reign of the Evil One. It is to align ourselves with the goodness of God and to seek to desire with our whole heart the will of God, recognizing that this requires the choice to stand against all that opposes that divine will. To pray to resist temptation and to be delivered from evil is to pray to have our consciences awoken and our awareness of the systemic evils in which we are all enmeshed sharpened, and to make the daily choice to align ourselves with the way of Jesus. We cannot walk the way of Jesus without facing resistance and opposition: both from within ourselves as well as from external sources. We cannot walk the way of Jesus in our own power but only in the strength and courage of the One who calls us, who will not lead us into temptation but protect us from the evils that we can easily fall prey to. Our own temptations may be very different from those besetting Jesus and the early disciples, and may appear more subtle and less clear-cut, but they are nonetheless very real. The temptation to prioritize our own comfort and well-being, for example, over the well-being of the poor and of the earth itself, is a daily temptation for many of us, and one we often do not even recognize. The temptation to use what power and influence we have to bolster up our own power and that of our immediate kith and kin, our nation or our own class or ethnic group, is one that must be resisted if we are to be true to the calling of Jesus to love our neighbour as our self and thereby love God with all our heart, soul and mind.

At the same time as the kindom of God faces us with stark choices, a further temptation we need to resist is that of projecting evil on to others in a desire to be identified with the good and the pure. Discerning the right action in any given situation is far from simple, and there may not be one right or wrong choice but a multiplicity of ambivalent options, no one of which is wholly pure or uncompromised. To recognize within ourselves the complexity of our own moral commitments is to recognize that we have the capacity for great good *and* evil, and that we will never entirely exorcise from ourselves the deadly sins of hatred, avarice, jealousy, lust and so on. It is all too easy to project the evil within ourselves that we cannot accept on to the other, and to turn them into the enemy. This may be one of many temptations we seek to pray against in solidarity with Jesus, who welcomed all into his kindom, including the very ones who would betray him.

The prayer of deliverance can take many forms and is as ancient as humanity. The Bible is full of the cries of God's little ones for deliverance from illness, poverty, enemy attack, abandonment, old age and much more besides. Our own prayers for deliverance may chime with many of these ancient prayers, but will take on their own specific details, themes and texture. Some of the prayers that follow were written in the time of Covid, during which the cry to be delivered from evil rose from millions of lips throughout the world and took on a very particular hue. At the beginning of lockdown, in March 2020, I often woke in the middle of the night and, unable to go back to sleep, would creep downstairs to the living room, light the candles and sit with the cats on the sofa, praying the night office and thereby participating in the struggle against the powers and principalities which has marked the prayer of the Church since its inception. The ancient vigil of the night, maintained by many hermits and monastics since earliest times, is a time when the struggle against evil, pain, suffering and being overwhelmed takes on a particularly intense quality, without the distractions of daylight tasks and priorities. Many of us have experienced how the pains of our own individual and collective lives, whether physical, spiritual or emotional, can draw us deeper into an identification with Jesus' prayer in Gethsemane and with the wrestling of all those who pray, out of anguish, for deliverance.

Deliver us from evil

After Evelyn Underhill

Abba Amma,
deliver us from evil – not from the pain and trial
which test and brace us,
but from all that can damage our relation to you.

Do not let us be swamped
in the strange tumult and conflict,
the evil that results from the clash of wills
unharmonized with your will.

Deliver us by keeping clear
that single relation with you
which is our peace.

Deliver us from our share in the world's sin,
our twist away from holiness,
reinforcing by your energetic grace
our feeble will towards the good.

Amma Abba,
in constantly returning to you,
Absolute Love, may we find
the sovereign remedy against temptation
and defence against the assaults of the world's ills.

Judas

You could have barred him
from the table
but you did not.

You could have shamed him
in front of the others
but you did not.

You could have refused
his kiss, averted your eyes
from his gaze.

You took it full in the face.
You did not protect
your body from the blow.

You permitted him to do
what he did, plotting the deed
as he reclined on your shoulder.

We demonized him.
You did not.

We othered him
and cast him out from our midst
in our need of a villain.

We refuse to recognize
the complexity of his deed,
of what we daily do.

Litany for hard times

From apathy and acedia
Amma Abba, deliver us

From despair and dejection
Amma Abba, deliver us

From the noonday demon in the midday sun
Amma Abba, deliver us

From hankering after the place we have left
Amma Abba, deliver us

From all assaults of the mind and body
Amma Abba, deliver us

From the pain that wakes us in the dead of night
Amma Abba, deliver us

From the terror that grips our heart and robs us of peace
Amma Abba, deliver us

From the arrogance and hubris that separates us from
    your love
Amma Abba, deliver us

From the self-pity and self-destruction that unmake your
    work in us
Amma Abba, deliver us

From the lust that drives us to possess and the greed that
    hankers after more
Amma, Abba, deliver us

From absorption in trivia and distraction in what does
not matter
Amma Abba, deliver us

From lack of care for our neighbour, the orphan, the widow
and the refugee
Amma Abba, deliver us

From the blunting of wonder that prevents us from worship
Amma Abba, deliver us

From the evil that seeks to destroy what is good
Amma Abba, deliver us

From the grief that will not be comforted and the sorrow that
we cling to
Amma Abba, deliver us

Psalm from the abyss

Abba Amma
I am yours
save me

Lift me up from the swirling waters
that threaten to take my life

Save me from the raging storm
that beats at my door

The waves are up to my neck
the icy blast knocks me sideways

The current pulls me downwards to death
The salt fills my mouth so that I cannot breathe

My life founders on the abyss
The roar of your waterfalls goes over me

You have cradled me since my birth
Do not let my life go down to the pit

Reach into the depths and lift me up in your strong arms
Bring me out of the watery deeps and set me high upon a rock

Abba Amma
You have made me
My life is in your hands

If I die, I die to you
If I live, I live to you

In life and death
My lips shall praise you

Prayer of an ageing woman

Abba	Amma
I am ageing	bear me
I am hurting	heal me
I am smarting	soothe me
I am scattered	gather me
I am fractured	repair me
I am grieving	comfort me
I am wounded	salve me
I am bleeding	staunch me
I am weeping	hold me
I am ageing	carry me

4 a.m. prayer

when sleep deserts my wakeful brain
when pain assails me in the dark

Abba Amma

when Donald is in his room
and all the candles are lit

Amma Abba

when Hannah is exhausted from her seventy-four-hour labour
when Lucy May wakes for her feed

Abba Amma

when the sisters rise for Vigils
in the silent hour before dawn

Amma Abba

when Richard lies grieving his beloved Evelyn
when Judith can't fly from Melbourne to her father's grave

Abba Amma

when the lilac and the tulips bloom in the grate
and the mourning women keep watch

Amma Abba

when night is banished in the Queen Elizabeth wards
and another patient fights for breath

Abba Amma

when the rest of the world's asleep
and the cats curl beside me in my lonely prayer

Amma Abba

Pain

It comes and goes
like the rain:

none for days, and then
a deluge from the skies

battering the earth,
soaking the body's ground.

It swells to a crescendo
like the growing light,

seeping into the
still dark room.

It has got me up early
to light the candles,

seeking words like charms
to ease its dull monotone.

The sisters at Malling
will be up at prayer

in the grey chapel,
voices rising with the dawn.

Most of them are old
and many now have gone.

They live with pain daily
yet rarely speak of it.

Every day is a fresh
assault against the

passing of their life,
the dying of the light.

It will come, it will go.
But ah, the glory

that rises to a crescendo
singing, singing.

Lullaby

in sleep you carry me
in rest you rock me
in sitting you sit with me

in waiting you watch with me
in gazing you look at me
in stilling you centre me

in silence you speak in me
in solitude you meet me
in emptiness you fill me

in gentleness you strengthen me
in quiet you quicken me
in trust you save me

in breathing you breathe through me
in bearing you bear with me
in being you live in me

in ageing you grow with me
in slowing you settle me
in dying you rise in me

Prayer for deliverance

Abba Amma
when I am tempted to despair
remind me of your promises more numerous than the sand

Amma Abba
when I despise myself or another
remind me of your good work in me and all your creatures

Abba Amma
when I am too tired to begin again
rouse me from my fatigue with your Spirit's energy

Amma Abba
when I no longer savour the beauty of this world
waken me again to its manifold wonders

Abba Amma
when I cease to care
stir in me your deep desire

Amma Abba
when I cloud your image in me with indifference
shake me from my listlessness and restore me to your glory

Abba Amma
when I wander off in the wilderness
send your pillar of cloud to lead me

Amma Abba
when I am faint and famished
feed me with honey from the rock

Abba Amma
when I am lost in the dark wood of my pilgrimage
guide me through the slough of despond and bring me
    safely home

Remove the cup

Abba Amma, remove the cup.
I cannot drink it.

Remove the cup.
You are asking too much.

Remove the cup.
I did not sign up for this.

Remove the cup.
I want to walk away.

Remove the cup.
I want to look away.

I cannot bring myself
to gaze on what is happening.

Remove the cup.
It is too bitter, it is too much.

How many millions must share
your agonizing death

alone, fighting for breath,
before this cup is drained?

Grenfell Tower lament

Where were you in the torrent and the fire
in the towering inferno?

I called to you for aid but you did not answer
I screamed to you for rescue but you were asleep

with the Kensington millionaires in their silk sheets
secure in their insulated apartments

Were you caught off guard with the councillors whose
    money-scraping
left us at the mercy of the flammable cladding?

Where were you in the torrent and the fire
in the towering inferno?

No, you were suffocating with us in the acrid smoke
choking on the fumes, clawing at the windows to get out

You came to us in the firefighters risking life and limb
to get some few of us out alive

You came to us in the outpouring of goodness, pity and anger
from neighbours who rushed to the scene with food, clothing
    and money

You came to us in the aging monarch who insisted on visiting
in the politicians who took to the streets

You suffered with us, died with us
you survived with us and will rise with us

Every day you wake with us to relive the memories
Every day you stand with us at the public meetings to
    clamour for justice

Every day you carry us on the shoulders of strangers
and sing to us in the songs of school children

A litany of struggle and remembrance

First voice   Wandering for years in the wilderness
looking for a way out

Second voice footsore
parched throats
sunstroke
hardened skin
clothes worn thin

Third voice   going round in circles
chafing at the bit
bored with limited rations
angry with our leaders
irritated with each other
forgetting where we've come from
losing the sense of where we are going

First voice   Some of our mothers died in the desert
bones bleached by sun
unremembered graves

Second voice Others went mad with the waste of it
patience worn to the bone

Third voice   Some wrested power for themselves
refusing to wait for scraps from the master's
table

First voice   Others absconded   abandoned the caravan trail
headed off on their own up isolated ravines
seeking an oasis

Second voice We hear snatches of their stories
but much is lost   scattered in the desert sands
snatched up by the wind and blown away

We remember the ones we knew or heard tell of

Third voice	women who refused to give up on their calling
	who had a sense of our common destiny to
	share a sacred priesthood
	who led the way when few were ready to follow

First voice   women who kept vigil
protecting the embers of the fire of God's
smouldering passion
who spoke out against restriction, limitation,
small and mean vision
who took their elders to task
shamed them   demanded something better

Second voice women who hunkered down for the long haul
who prayed their way through refusal,
ignorance, resistance
who found the means to inspire and nourish
sons and daughters
when they had been offered little themselves

Third voice   women who heckled and complained and insisted
when many around them demanded they keep
silent
women with bold, expansive dreams and
theologies to match

First voice   women who clung to the hem of the garments
of healing
refusing to let go
who wrested a blessing from their opponents
who blazed a trail for others to follow

Second voice women too numerous to name
even when their names have been remembered

We remember them
We mourn them and celebrate them
We take hold of their boldness and courage
We are here because of all they have dared and hoped
   and believed
We will not fail them now

7

Prayers From the Desert

In the fourth and fifth centuries of the Christian era, as Christianity became established as the religion of the Roman Empire and took on more of the trappings of worldly power and privilege, an extraordinary exodus began to take place, as men and women left the big cities and centres and took up residence in the deserts of Egypt. It has been estimated that as many as 40,000 were involved in this movement, although the numbers of solitary hermits, the abbas and ammas of the desert, were much smaller. Nevertheless, they have had an influence on Christian tradition far beyond their size. Living lives of remote austerity in clusters of solitary cells, they formed an unlikely foundation for the monasticism which would grow from their roots and flourish across Europe. They devoted themselves to solitary prayer and the simplest of manual labour, tasks that were repeated again and again to aid the processes of prayer. Speaking rarely, and writing nothing themselves, those who went out to the desert in search of their spiritual wisdom gathered stories and sayings about these abbas and ammas which are not widely known but hugely prized for their humanity, compassion, humour and wisdom by those who know them. They breathe the sharp air and searing light of desert expanses, the extremes of cold and heat, the merciless glare of the sun and the exquisite explosion of stars in the night sky, all of which were intimately known by Jesus on his own retreats into the desert for prayer, where he wrestled with the devil and with temptation.

The lives and sayings of the desert abbas and ammas, and the desert landscape itself, therefore throw much light on the Prayer of Jesus to his Abba father. They take us into the austerity and expansiveness of the landscape of prayer, to which we are invited to come, if we dare. They take us back to the core simplicity at the heart of Jesus' prayer, and to the fundamental values of charity, radical trust, love of neighbour and whole-hearted dedication to God which the gospel demands. I have stolen shamelessly from these sayings and stories in the prayers that follow, almost all of which follow closely the translation in Yushi Nomura's gender-inclusive version, *Desert Wisdom* (accompanied by wonderful pen and ink drawings which, themselves, offer powerful and often humorous commentary on the texts). Apart from one or two, they are, then, essentially 'found' prayers or poems, although the arrangement of each is my own. I have tried to keep the brevity and simplicity of the original in my prayers, a discipline which I have found enormously liberating, as someone who routinely over-writes and has to hack and hack my poetry and prose back, in the editing stage, until it occasionally achieves the compression and clarity of good writing. Paradoxically, the constraint of keeping to the spirit and style of the desert abbas' and ammas' own terse, well-chosen words, freed my writing to become much simpler and more pared down. And prayer, too, need not be wordy or full of explanation and commentary. God who formed us and knows us more intimately than we know ourselves, who counts the hairs on our heads and collects our tears in her bottle, hardly needs us to explain what is in our hearts or minds. I hope that these prayers may encourage us all to offer fewer rather than more words to God, yet with the expansive silence and sighs, the tears and laughter, which doubtless accompanied the desert abbas' and ammas' prayers.

Arriving

Abba Amma.
I wait a long time in your presence.

Amma Abba.
I sit at the door of your entrance.

Abba Amma.
I come with my overwhelming baggage.

Amma Abba.
I long to divest myself of my encumbrance.

Abba Amma.
For a long time you refuse my advances.

Amma Abba.
Your sternness overcomes your tenderness.

Abba Amma.
Your tenderness overcomes your sternness.

Amma Abba.
A word is growing out of your wilderness.

Abba Amma.
Place the stone of your silence in every orifice.

The absence of God

Abba Amma
You have gone a long way from me.

You left the city with its passageways and thoroughfares
for the secret spaces of the desert crevices.

Amma Abba
I hunger for your presence as a pelican in the wilderness.

I have paced the dark streets of my memories
searching for signs of your kindness.

You have taken yourself away from me.
Only the lingering scent of your fragrance

is suspended in the air, as the moon,
a huge pale orb luminous with an absence

more terrible than the presence
of an army of lovers.

To be set alight

Abba, Amma,
as much as I am able

I practise my small rule,
a little fasting,
some prayer and meditation.

I remain quiet.
As much as I am able
I keep my thoughts clean.

What else should I do?

Ah, that you would
make my whole life flame!

To assist a sister or brother

Amma Abba
when my brother
falls asleep at his prayer

give me the grace
not to wake him
but to cradle his sleeping head

in my hands
and thus to let him rest.

When my sister
grows forgetful
at her work

give me the grace
not to scold her
but to assist gently

in the task she has forgotten
and thus complete the work.

Abiding in the cell

Abba Amma
here we are
in our little cells

each one alone
for a season
and a day.

Teach us
not to fret
but to accept

this unlooked-for
Sabbath
graciously.

Teach us
the truth of the gospel
in our little cell.

To bear fruit

Amma Abba
let me not be
all words
with no work

like a tree
with leaves
but no fruit.

Let me first
do good works
and thus produce
good words

like a tree
that bears fruit
and is also leafy.

Prayer for simplicity

Abba Amma
let me live
a simple life

When I am hungry
may I eat

When I am thirsty
may I drink

When I am cold
may I light the fire

When I am hot
may I find the tree's shade

When I am tired
may I rest

When I awake
may I work

And may I speak evil
of no living thing

Thus may I be saved

Those who hurt us

Amma Abba
teach me how to
do good to those
who hurt me

and when I
cannot
do that much

take me far
away from
the one who
has wronged me

and teach me
to keep
my mouth shut.

Rising, falling

Abba Amma
this is my life

I rise up, I fall down
I rise up, I fall down
I rise up, I fall down

Abba Amma
Have mercy

The daily round

Amma Abba

day after day
I sit at my work

I get up from
my work to pray

I sit down
at my work again

I get up again
to pray

and thus
I spend my day

until it is time
to sleep

I get up and sit down
I get up and sit down

I rise
I pray

I work
I sleep

and thus may I be saved

The grief that is useful

Abba Amma
give to me the grief that is useful

that I may weep over my own faults
and those of my neighbour

and thus attach myself
to the perfect good.

Deliver me from the grief
that comes from the enemy

that is full of mockery
and some call accidie.

By prayer and psalmody
I pray you to cast this spirit out.

Knowing when to speak

Amma Abba
teach me when to speak
and when to be silent

when to accept
the invitation to words
and when to decline

that I may inspire others
as much by my silence
as by what I say

and when I speak
may my mouth utter
what is in my heart

Love without judgement

Abba Amma
teach me to be
like this dog
who, like me,
has much love
but, unlike me,
never passes judgement
on its owner
and is thus
the happier of
the two of us.

Prayer for patience

Amma, make me like the mother bird
who sits patiently on her eggs in the nest
abiding all the stretches of boredom
until the first egg cracks
and her newborn chicks emerge.

Ah, how I long for the boredom
and nothingness of my little cell!
And when they come, I'm impatient to be off,
like the bird abandoning her eggs.

This day's labour

Amma Abba
sweeten
this day's labour
with song.
For unless
the mind sings
with the body
our labour
is in vain.

And if I cannot
or will not sing
let my window
be open
to the song
of the birds
and the bees
that their music
may be
like honey
on my tongue.

For a hard heart

Abba Amma
soften our hard hearts
with your tender word

that they may yield
to your wisdom

as the hardest rock
gives way, over time
to water.

To keep God's commandments

Amma Abba,
show me when
it is necessary
to break
the commandment
made by people
in order to keep
the commandment
of God.
And give me
the courage
to do it.

A teachable spirit

Like young branches
that are malleable
and can be corrected
and staked to grow
where they will be
most useful
and most beautiful

so teach my spirit
to be bendable
and mendable
ready to be corrected
and to grow
straight and true –
even if my aging bones
cannot do the same.

To accept the human lot

Abba Amma,
how I long to be free from care,
not to work
but to worship you
without interruption.

Yet I am human
and as long as I live
I must work.

Teach me to accept
my need to labour
my need to pray
my need to rest.

Only in heaven
shall I worship you
without ceasing
neither resting nor labouring.

To be delivered from folly

Amma Abba,
the time is here
of which Abba Anthony spoke

when people are insane
and attack those who are sane

because they do not think like them
or vote like them
or act like them.

Lead us not into their ways
and deliver us from their madness.

Prayer against the weariness of words

Abba Amma,
here I am again
with my words
battering at your door.

They are heavy,
like Abba Agathon's pebble,
and I cannot seem to
put them down for long.

I'll be lucky
if I manage
three hours
of silence

whereas he
carried his pebble
in his mouth
for three years.

I pity you
who must be
as weary as I am
with my words.

If you will help me,
I will try to desist
for a while.

Prayer against the weariness of others

Amma Abba
I am weary of the company of others
Save me from their clamouring

I am exhausted by their talk
I am drained by their noise
I am overwhelmed by their demands

O that I had in the desert
a traveller's lodging place
that I might leave my people and go away from them

Take me away
like a dove in the cleft of the rock
Set me up on the rock that is higher than I

The well in the wilderness

Abba Amma
You are the sweet well
for the one who thirsts
in the desert

It is closed
to those who speak
but open
to those who are silent

Amma Abba
I come in silence
Let me find the well

Prayer for the midday sun

Lord, it is hot.
The sun beats down
and the cat is asleep
under the hedge.
The plants
in their pots
are wilting.
And so am I.

In the midday heat,
soothe my parched throat
with your cool
water of life.
Let my limbs
rest easy
and forgive
my afternoon nap.

8

Canticle of the Creatures

Do the creatures of the earth pray, as well as humans? The biblical writers clearly thought so, as they frequently enjoin all of creation to join in the praise of the creator. The psalms, in particular, endlessly offer worship and praise from the wide created earth: sun and moon, sky and stars, rain and cloud, winds and storms, snow and frost, earth and sea creatures, day and night, cold and heat each echo in their own distinctive voice the glory and magnificence of the creator. As the begin ning of Psalm 19 puts it:

> The heavens are telling the glory of God;
> and the firmament proclaims God's handiwork.
> Day to day pours forth speech,
> and night to night declares knowledge.
> There is no speech, nor are there words;
> their voice is not heard;
> yet their voice goes out through all the earth,
> and their words to the end of the world.
> (Psalm 19.1–4)

The psalmist wrestles with the paradox that, although the heavens and the earth do not 'speak' with words or speech which humans can understand, and thus 'their voice is not heard', yet they have their own language, their own characteristic and unique form of speech which God hears and comprehends: 'their voice goes out through all the earth, and their words to the end of the world'. And perhaps, if humans attuned their ears really to listen to the voices of all the earth's creatures, we too might hear and comprehend what they are saying.

The conceit of this chapter is that the creatures do, indeed, address God, each in their own creaturely way, with their own creaturely voices. Inspired by Jen Hadfield's fabulous poem, 'Paternoster', in which she offers a horsey version of the Lord's Prayer, complete with neighs and pleas for good mash and oats, I have imagined a range of creatures and parts of the landscape offering their own versions of the prayer. These improvisations might make the reader smile, but the intent is deadly serious: to engender respect for every living creature on the earth and to elicit our care of the earth creatures, as well as to invite human readers to improvise in their prayer with as much freedom and creativity as the creatures surely do. After a handful of fairly close improvisations on the Lord's Prayer, other prayers and poems follow where there is less resemblance to the form of the prayer but where river, sea, daylight and growing things simply offer their prayer by being what they are, creatures reflecting the glory and wonder of their creator. And these creaturely offerings teach me, too, how to pray; so the chapter ends by coming back to my own prayer, in company and harmony with the prayer of the whole created order. Thus all that follows is in the spirit of St Francis' 'canticle of the creatures', in which Francis calls on all of creation, as his brothers and sisters, to join his praise of the divine: 'May you be praised, my Lord, with all your creatures.'

And all creation cries in a loud voice, 'Amen'.

The cat's prayer

There is little we need and we will not
beg for it. Take your wicker basket away,
we'd rather sleep in a box
or perch on the corner of a new rug.

Give us our daily Felix,
fresh cooked chicken or fish
and on Sundays a sliver of roast beef
or lamb shank. Keep our litter tray
clean. Do not obstruct the cat flap
and, if we should bring in
a juicy shrew or mouse from the garden,
save your pity. Deliver us
from the window cleaners' clattering
ladder. Do not lead us by deception
into the indignity of the cat carrier.
Preserve us from the vet's sharp needle.

There is nothing to forgive us.
For ours is the power, the glory and the majesty.
For ever and ever, purr without end.
Amen.

The dog's prayer

My master, at your table,
my eyes must tell you
how I adore you.
Or my thumping tail.
I'll follow no other.
All I need is one look
and with a bound
I'm here, ready
to leap out that door.
Or, if not a walk,
give me a bone,
a juicy bone!
I'll overlook every
missed walk for a bone.

You can lead me
up and down
the highways and byways
of earth and of heaven,
and I will follow,
catching the ball
of your attention,
flung far and wide,
and bringing it home
to your feet.
As often as you throw it
high in the air,
I'll be there!

What does
that pesky cat
know
of such loyalty
and love?

I'm yours,
for ever and ever.

The sheep's prayer

Great Shepherd over the mountain,
Our Lady of the lambs:
hear the prayer we offer.

Give us this day our wool to warm us
a wide field, plenty of grass to feed us
still pools to water us.

Let there be a company of sheep
scattered around the hillside
and our little ones near us.

Let us be left alone for a long time.
Come rain, come sun, let our bodies
shiver, sweat, drip, fatten, wetten.

Deliver us from the farmer's van.
May our lambs grow old beside us.

Let the hard places be in our hooves.
Let the running streams be in our dreams.
Let the skies reflect in our eyes.

Let us become field and wind and weather.
Shelter us for ever and ever.

The donkeys' prayer

They had no use for us
this year, the year of the lockdown.

No crowds, no waving of palms,
no processions.

We're used to being overlooked.
Passers-by fuss over the pretty ponies.

We stay in the corner of the field,
heads bowed, bearing the shame.

They've never had much use for you,
either, for all the hullabaloo and shouting.

They pushed you out
to a stinking rubbish tip,

strung you up and waited
for your body to gasp its last.

But we carried you:
once at the beginning

in your mother's arms,
and again on your final entry to the city.

Though they have forgotten us,
we will not forget you.

Should you need us again,
our backs are ready to bear the weight.

The blackbird's prayer

In my sleek black coat
from my orange beak

I sing to you

From the top of the silver birch
at dawn, at dusk

I sing to you

With all the art of my song
and the cream of my heart

I sing to you

To win your love
to praise my God

I sing to you

Throughout the spring
while the earth kindles

I sing to you

In rain, in wind, in sun
while the season's barely begun

I sing to you

I'll trill
and thrill
and spill my song
all day long

'Til there's nothing
left to sing

Yet still I'll sing to you

The primroses' prayer

After Christopher Smart

with a pure heart and a face open as the sun we pray to you
with raindrops on our petals we mirror the sky

in our lives' briefest spell, we hold nothing back
and you will not spurn our offering

you will inhale our delicate perfume
you will not crush the life out of us before our petals wilt and fall

you will rejoice in our lemon-yellow dresses
and the pale cream satin skirts of our neighbours

for the Lord made a nosegay in the meadow with his disciples
and surely the primrose and violet were in it and all the plants
    of the woods

for the flowers have their angels and their wings are the
    colours of spring
and even Solomon in all his glory was not clothed as one
    of these

for flowers are peculiarly the poetry of Christ
who gazed on the lilies of the field and was drunk with
    their beauty

for the right names of flowers are yet in heaven
and we shall hear our names called after our brief spell
    on earth

and we shall cry 'Glory! Glory! Hallelujah!' when we join
the chorus of stamen and petals lifting up their voices to Christ

who walks in Eden at the cool of day and plucks the roses
    of Sharon
and the bees will gather nectar and offer their honey to heaven

The rivers' prayer

From the highest crags and mountain passes,
from deep underground caves we come,
our waters rushing, gathering, gurgling,
praising the one source.
All that would impede our way we carry
before us: sticks, stones, leaves, debris.
We cover what remains with cold forgetfulness,
our watery semblance of forgiveness.
We have no intention to hurt but our power
when resisted will maim, snap, fell and founder.
Do not take our currents for evil or anger:
they are simply the way our energy flows.

Human and beast may drink from our ledges,
siphon our surplus to irrigate crops,
cool heaving furnaces, cleanse industry's residues.
Yet we are not immune from your poisons,
our once-sweet waters are now brackish
with thousands of your spillages.
Depleted but not diminished we rush on,
never ceasing our murmuring for mercy.
On and on we go, brooking no refusal,
bearing earth's gashes and wounds
until we reach our goal: to merge
with the great ocean from whence we came

Source beyond source
Depth beyond all depths
Darkness gathering all darkness
Abyss unfathomable.

The sea's prayer

The sea is our mother
     she has birthed us
     and will carry us

The sea is our teacher
     she will instruct us in the way
     to walk on her shifting sands

The sea is our healer
     in her waters we find cool balm
     and the cauterizing of our wounds

The sea is our lover
     she draws us into deep waters
     of passion and embrace

The sea is our longest journey
     our destination   voyage
     and our final home

The road to the isles

The rise of the wave, and the fall.
The silence. The call.

The island and the sea.
The return journey.

The draw of the edge.
The lure of the ledge.

The cloister, the machair.
Open skies. Hidden lair.

The surge, the surf.
The bog, the turf.

The wheeling birds' cries.
The winds' replies.

The road to the isles, and back.
The body's fullness and slack.

The island in the world, in me.
The endless return journey.

Aldeburgh

I come seeking words but also its many textured silences.
Olive green and purple of marram grass and sedge swaying
   along the marches.
Sludge and crunch of dirty seawater crashing on the pebbles,
my boots pressing and heaving slowly up the shore.
Seabirds crying out along the horizon,
wide skies whitening into the distance.

The Benjamin Britten memorial window in the parish church,
is a rush and boom of colour: brilliant purples, aqua of
   the river,
the silver white of the curlew hovering over creation,
flaming reds and oranges of the burning fiery furnace,
brilliant velvet blue of the night sky, picked out with sparks
   and stars.

The rising of the dark, blankets of fog sweeping in off the
   North Sea.
Skies of slate jet, lights coming on across the scattered town
as I trudge the shingle back from Thorpeness.

I might say I came for prayer and poetry, for seascapes and
   skyscapes,
the glittering, meandering river curling up through the mudflats.
The place pulls me back to itself in spite of what it is I came for,
rinses me clean of too much thought and clutter,
washes out the primary colours (anything too bold or obvious)
and gives me back a palette of ochre, dun, dull mauves,
   dusty browns.

Give me your emptiness, Aldeburgh. A quality of openness.
   Your skies, seas, land reaching off into nowhere
   the way sound goes on for ever,
a turning into the darkness,
a time without judgement or harshness:
autumn's inscrutable purposes.

Sunday morning at the abbey

In the night rain
while I slept heavy in my bed

The nuns singing Lauds
bright sound against a pewter sky

Later, church bells pealing
light plays shadow games on the grass

I sip my bitter coffee slowly
read poems by Rumi and Kabir

I have been here many times
in this garden of soul-making, hidden behind high walls

but never, until now, this chair, this light,
these bells, this rain-drenched morning

Our mother mountain

Sheep's Head Peninsula

Our mother mountain
Ballyroon Rosskerric
who art in heaven

Give us today your pure air
grant us the sunlight to warm us, wind to cool us
fresh water in the rain-swollen streams to refill our bottles

Give us our soda bread cheese sandwich
forgive us our cross words
and teach us the peaceable way

Lead us along the well-signed path
strengthen us for the next ridge
let all the stiles be secure

Bring us out of the boggy marshes
pick us up when we stumble
and deliver us from sudden mists and driving rain

For yours is the beauty and splendour
the ever-changing glory
of this hidden peninsula

which time and tides have forgotten
where we hope to return
for ever and ever. Amen.

9

For Yours Is The Kindom,
The Power and The Glory

The doxology which most of us are used to including in the
Lord's Prayer – 'for yours is the kingdom, the power and the
glory, for ever and ever' – is not an original part of the prayer
and does not appear in either Luke's or Matthew's version,
although there is a shortened form of it in the Didache, where
the prayer ends 'since it is your might and glory into the ages'.
The use of the doxology in English dates from at least 1549,
when we find it in the First Prayer Book of Edward VI, which
was itself influenced by William Tyndale's New Testament
translation of 1526. Many contemporary scholars, and certainly many feminists, regard the doxology as somewhat in
tension with the content of the prayer itself, since it seems to
endorse a form of patriarchal power, along with kingship, that
is antithetical to the spirit and teaching of Jesus.

I wondered, then, about including any reference to it at all
in this book, but the beauty about improvisations is that one
can riff off an original in any direction and even undermine
what seem to be dominant meanings or associations in the
original (or originals). I decided to use the doxology as a way
of placing the Abba Amma prayer within the context of ending
and endings and, most particularly, that most ultimate horizon
and unmaking of death, against which all human endeavour,
including prayer, is conducted. I hope that the prayers that follow do not endorse patriarchal or hierarchical ways of thinking
and praying but invite those who pray to face into their own
ultimate demise along with the death of all their plans, projects
and possessions. Alongside prayers which face into that ultimate horizon of unknowing, death, there are also prayers which

acknowledge our absolute dependence on the Spirit of God for the very act of praying, as well as existing. Somehow, facing into the hope that God's glory may be revealed in our own passing, we discover all the more how we cannot pray one word, we cannot breathe one breath, except as it comes from God, source of all life and being as well as the goal towards which our lives move. Reflecting on our death takes us back to reconsider our life and to acknowledge our dependence for everything – breath, life, food, prayer, faith – upon God who is both Alpha and Omega, beginning and end of all we are and all there is that exists.

If we have prayed the Prayer of Jesus in a spirit of poverty, simplicity and faithfulness, we shall surely discover that the invitation to face into our own death is not a fearful thing but a welcoming and freeing invitation into a new horizon beyond anything we can currently see or know or grasp. All human kingdoms and powers may ultimately come to dust, but the beauty, goodness and glory of God, in which we are each invited to participate, shall endure and welcome us home. In that knowledge, we may learn to live more freely, more trustingly, more openly, more joyfully and thus may return to the daily tasks and challenges set before us more trustingly, more faithfully, accepting every day that brings us closer to that last/ first great day of our awakening in and through the gate of death. The final prayer of this chapter, and of the book as a whole, takes us back to the daily, the arising each morning to begin a new day as if it were the first, or the last, in creation. And within the practice of our daily faith, the Prayer of Jesus keeps its central place and teaches us all we need to know of prayer, faith and life.

The kindom, the power and the glory

After Evelyn Underhill

Abba Amma,
yours is the kindom,
the power and the glory.

Yours is the kindom,
hidden from our sight
yet already present

your secret rule
working from within

your unseen pattern
imposed on our chaos

your spirit brooding on the deep
turning all things to your purpose.

Yours is the power,
inexhaustible energy
streaming forth from your hidden Being

by which the universe
visible and invisible
is sustained.

Yours is the glory,
the self-revealed splendour
of the eternal filling and transcending creation

seen in its humblest beauties
yet never fully known.

Amma Abba,
yours is the kindom,
the power and the glory.

You are the beginning
and the end of the soul's life.

One word

There is only one word, which all our words are praying
There is only one cry, which all our cries are saying

The one breath breathes through every word
The one Spirit hovers over all our prayers, quickening bird

All our words to silence finally come
All our prayers, on the Spirit's wing, find their way home

Back to the heart of God who bears us
Into the body of God who births us
Within the mystery of God who receives us

Our source
Our life
Our end

Abba Amma, amen.

Deo gratias

This is the work of these days:
throwing the window wide open
letting light and air in

sifting, shedding, sorting
attending, fingering gently
the pain that asks to be noticed

finding the place within
from which to let go
walking the way of dispossession

This is the work to be done
in gratitude and gladness
forgoing the big stick, the grandiose gesture

It does not have to be all
or nothing, it can be simply
what is needful in this moment

the patch of ground that invites
me to weed in the good morning hour
the body's call to rest in the drowsy afternoon

the single poem or chapter in a book
that desires my gift of time
my mind and body's attention

even while I bow in gratitude
for all the books and poems and hours
and flowers to come

Prayer for radical trust

For Donald

Abba Amma, the one we know and never know:
teach us to live gently with the unknowing
even as it grows deeper and stranger with the years

Amma Abba, whose love has held us
in places and ways we will never know:
teach us to trust in the holding
even when we fear it will unravel

Abba Amma, whose profound trust in us
allows us to let go of all we suppose we must be and become:
teach us to trust in the unmaking

Amma Abba, whose outpoured life demonstrates
the giving at the heart of all loving:
teach us not to cling to what we love
so that, in dispossessing,
we may find our heart's deepest desire
and rest there in true contentment

Abba Amma
        in the holding
        in the unknowing
        in the trust and the letting go
may we enter more deeply into your Triune life
and share your work of forming, bearing and loving.

The Spirit prays

Without your touch
we cannot move

Without your breath
we cannot live

Without your life
we cannot pray

Without your love
we cannot love

Teach us to pray

Abba Amma
we do not know how to pray
teach us

We do not dare to pray
strengthen us

We do not care to pray
inspire us

In your Spirit
teach us
touch us
talk with us
toil with us
speak with us
breathe in us
burn in us
enliven, enflame, embolden us

that we may speak with you
as friend speaks with friend

that we may gaze on you
as lovers gaze

that we may linger with you
as children linger

that we may run with you
as horses run

into the freedom and delight
of your kindom come

on earth as in heaven

Seeking the face of God

Abba Amma –
what would I give
to see your face?

You have given me
my whole life
to know you

whom I can never learn –
whose face
is veiled to me.

I catch glimpses
of your passing
as Moses did

hidden in the rock.
Let me see your face –
let me hear your voice.

Welcome, death

And death walks towards me with a light step,
strong and clear-eyed with a firm grip.

For she's an Amazon, a warrior, a soldier;
good country folk never fear the reaper

whose shrouded form is so well known
in these quiet lanes, flower-strewn,

to children, dogs, animals fed for slaughter,
every poor and rich man's son and daughter.

We may have failed to see her silent form,
camouflaged by fern and thorn.

We may have missed her muffled step
as through the lonely lanes she crept.

She does not come to rob or steal;
her touch will only soothe and heal.

She comes to infuse my ailing vigour
with her youthful ardour and candour.

Comfort and peace are in her hand
freely scattered throughout the land.

So I'll meet her gaze full in the eye,
step into her arms without a cry.

For she walks beside me all the way
longing and looking for this day.

Meditation

In sleep you carry me
In rest you rock me
In sitting you sit with me

In waiting you watch with me
In gazing you look at me
In stilling you centre me

In silence you speak in me
In solitude you meet me
In emptiness you fill me

In gentleness you strengthen me
In quiet you quicken me
In trust you save me

In breathing you breathe through me
In bearing you bear with me
In being you live in me

In ageing you grow with me
In slowing you settle me
In dying you rise in me

Prayer of the senses

Abba Amma
You have opened my ears
So that I may hear you

You have touched my lips
So that I may speak you

Abba Amma
You have opened my eyes
So that I may see you

You have touched my hands
So that I may hold you

Abba Amma
You have breathed in my nostrils
So that I may inhale you

You have blown on my face
So that I may feel you

Abba Amma
You have knocked on my heart
So that I may open to you

You have stirred my loins
So that I may yield to you

Abba Amma
You have opened my mouth
So that I may eat you

You have loosened my tongue
So that I may taste you

Coming to you

After Chagall's Tudeley windows

Up the ladder
of yellow light

I am coming to you

Resting in the wings
of the purple cherubim

I am coming to you

Flying into the waves
of the blue angel of death

I am coming to you

On the red horse
that gallops into night

I am coming to you

With my arms spread wide
looking back at what has passed

I am coming to you

Nestled in my mother's arms
on her pale baby breast

I am coming to you

Soaring up the fountain of love
diving into the whirlpool of light

I am coming, coming
I am coming to you

Potting out the sunflower

Every day,
make a fresh beginning,
as Abba Pior did.

You may be tired.
You may be hurting.
You may have forgotten
who you are
and where you're going.

No matter.
With the birds,
learn to sing again.
With the sun, rise,
travel across the sky.
With the roses,
bloom in beauty for a day
before you fade and drop.

Pick up your pen or hoe
with hope.
Face the blank page
of the rest of your life
with courage.

There is a poem
waiting to be written
that only you can write.
A song waiting to be sung
that only you can sing.
There is a sunflower
ready to be potted out
eager to climb the garden fence
and beam his enormous
orange smile.
It's your hands will do it.

Today is the day
to begin.

Notes and Sources

Chapter 1 Abba, Amma

'A mother's love' This prayer is made almost entirely of verbatim quotes from Julian of Norwich's *Revelations of Divine Love*. I am deeply grateful to the 1977 community at Lee Abbey, Devon (not far up the coast from my home in Higher Clovelly), where I spent a formative three months in my gap year, for introducing me to many new theological and liturgical resources and riches. Most particularly, Pamela Paul introduced me to Mother Julian when I was a young Christian who had never heard of any medieval mystic or known it was possible to address God as Mother. Pamela gave a series of talks to the resident community, in the little library overlooking Lee Bay, on a number of the medieval mystics, including Julian. I still have a rather battered copy of Clifford Woollard's Penguin translation of the *Revelations*, signed by the Kitchen team, of which I was a part, and which was a leaving present from them. More recently, I am grateful to Stephen Burns for introducing me, with much else besides, to Gail Ramshaw's Eucharistic Prayer after Julian of Norwich, in *Pray, Praise, and Give Thanks: A Collection of Litanies, Laments, and Thanksgivings at Font and Table* (Minneapolis, MN: Augsburg Fortress, 2017), pp. 72–3.

Chapter 2 Hallowed Be Your Name

Brian Wren's hymn, 'Bring many names', appears in *What Language Shall I Borrow?* (London: SCM Press, 2012, 2nd edn), pp. 137–8 as well as in the hymn collection *Bring Many*

Names: 35 New Hymns By Brian Wren (Carol Stream, IL: Hope Publishing Company, 1989), no 9.

The alternative first petition in the Lord's Prayer referred to here is mentioned by Gregory of Nyssa in *The Lord's Prayer, The Beatitudes*, ACW, vol. 18 (London: Longman, 1954), pp. 21–84 (52).

'Hallowed be your name' The term 'zhe' as a non-gendered form of address is becoming better known but may not be familiar to all readers.

'Praying the alphabet' This somewhat random offering of names for God all beginning with the letter 'a' is inspired by Gail Ramshaw's fabulous 'abecedary' in her *A Metaphorical God: An Abecedary of Images of God* (Chicago, IL: Liturgy Training Publications, 1995), in which she works her way through the entire alphabet offering an image of God for each letter, and even more by her chapter addressing God in terms all beginning with the letter 'W' in *Under the Tree of Life: The Religion of a Feminist Christian* (New York: Continuum, 1998), pp. 63–4. Once again, thanks to Stephen Burns for introducing me to Ramshaw's work. I loved the challenge of working through the first few pages of my *Concise Oxford Dictionary* and seeing whether and how terms could be applied to God. Some were easy and obvious: '*agape*', for instance, or 'abounding' and 'acquittal'; others were surprising yet instantly recognized as biblical, such as 'accuser', 'adversary' and 'alpha' itself (along with 'omega'). Yet others were entirely unknown to me, such as 'allogamy', which means the fertilization of a flower by pollen from another flower, and therefore can certainly become a divine name! I could have gone much further, but 'Amen' seemed a good place to stop. I love the prospect of working my way through the entire alphabet in what time remains to me and stretching my language and liturgy in unimaginable ways.

'God beyond binary' I am aware of a danger in using the composite 'Abba Amma' and its parallel, 'Amma Abba', in unwittingly reinforcing the gender binary: the very opposite of what I intend in this book! This prayer, as well as others, explicitly seeks to move beyond any such binary; its multiple triplets expand the terms and names for God until they (almost) explode into silence. No name can ever fully know the God who is never to be identified with any object in the world and to whom our language stutters 'no' as much as 'yes'.

'Our light and peace and joy' This prayer is based closely on a hymn by Symeon the New Theologian, *Hymns of Divine Love*, quoted in Gail Ramshaw, *God Beyond Gender* (Minneapolis, MN: Fortress, 1995), p. 112.

'Jesus my brother' I wrote this prayer shortly after the death of my brother, Ian, one year older than me, from whom most of the family was estranged for the larger part of Ian's life. I hope the prayer works without knowledge of the backcloth of my own life and relationship to my brother(s), but for me, the prayer is as much about him as it is about Jesus as a brother. The irony of the first line is deliberate: I have (or had) three brothers and none of them were able to be to me the brother I needed.

'Mother of the broken-hearted' Grandparents have been extremely important in my life and I am deeply fortunate to have had close relationships with all four grandparents. I have loved the address to God as 'grandfather' (and analogously, 'grandmother'), since I discovered it in an Ojibway prayer, 'Grandfather, look at our brokenness', https://rumisgarden.co.uk/blogs/traditional-meditations/ojibway-prayer-grandfather-look-at-our-brokenness (accessed 27.08.2021).

'Name above all names' For more on the notion of Jesus as Christa, see my *Seeking the Risen Christa* (London: SPCK, 2011), especially chapter 1.

'Friend of the world' Sallie McFague's work on the significance of metaphor and model in the naming and addressing of God is a major resource in contemporary feminist theology. Her *Models of God: Theology for an Ecological, Nuclear Age* (London: SCM Press, 1987) develops extensively the threefold models of God as Lover, Mother and Friend.

'I come to you' In this prayer, I seek to inhabit the Pauline notion that, as children of God, we are heirs and inheritors of the freedom of the household, in contrast to the bondage of slaves. See Galatians 4 and 5, particularly.

'God my clothing' Julian's imagery of God wrapping and clothing the beloved as a mother clothes an infant has always been one I have loved, but has recently taken on new resonance in light of work by David Tombs and others on the stripping and nakedness of Jesus at his crucifixion. See Jayme R. Reaves, David Tombs and Rocío Figueroa (eds), *When Did We See You Naked? Jesus as a Victim of Sexual Abuse* (London: SCM Press, 2021). To pray to God as both 'my nakedness' and 'my clothing' has new depths of meaning in light of the abuse which Jesus appears to have suffered in his flesh and his sexuality. Knowing and naming our own nakedness and our need to be clothed in the love of God is part of our journey in prayer which may require us to plumb the depths of our shame and our need for healing.

Chapter 3 Your Kindom Come, Your Will Be Done

Gail Ramshaw writes about 'the myth of the crown' in *God Beyond Gender*, p. 59.

Ada María Isasi Díaz, 'Kin-dom of God: A Mujerista Proposal', in Benjamin Valentin (ed.), *In Our Own Voices: Latino/a Renditions of Theology* (Maryknoll, NY: Orbis Books, 2010). See note 35 in Chapter 1 above. Stephen Cherry commends the use of 'kindom' in *Thy Will Be Done: The 2021 Lent Book* (London: Bloomsbury, 2020), pp. 58–61.

John Dominic Crossan explores the notion of the household as a metaphor for the rule of God in *The Greatest Prayer: Rediscovering the Revolutionary Message of the Lord's Prayer* (London: SPCK, 2011), chapters 2 and 4.

'God our affinity' Our belonging in God's household/family relativizes all other claims of blood, kinship, nationality or race.

'Bone of your bone' and 'The kindness of God' Both of these prayers draw extensively on concepts found in Julian of Norwich's theology. I am also indebted to Janet Martin Soskice's essay on Julian on 'The kindness of God' in her book of essays, *The Kindness of God: Metaphor, Gender, and Religious Language* (Oxford: Oxford University Press, 2007), chapter 7 (and the whole collection of essays is one I return to often for its wisdom).

'Prayer of the household' As above, I am indebted to Crossan's reading of the Lord's Prayer for the metaphor of the household which I seek to expand here.

'In the shepherd's fold' This prayer takes its inspiration from Crossan's reading of the metaphor of the shepherd through the lens of the smallholding, farm and household units which would have been familiar to Jesus' first hearers. See Crossan, *The Greatest Prayer*, chapter 2.

'Looking towards the promised land' This piece could be read by a variety of different voices, or antiphonally, with the first line of each couplet read by one or more voices and the second line by everyone else.

Chapter 4 Give Us Today Our Daily Bread

The quotation from Gregory of Nyssa is from Hilda Graef's translation of *The Lord's Prayer, The Beatitudes* (New York: Paulist Press, 1954), p. 67. It is quoted by Cherry in *Thy Will Be Done*, pp. 76–7.

I am indebted to Ash Cocksworth for the reference to Augustine's regard for the Lord's Prayer as a 'sacrament of the faithful'. This can be found in Augustine's letter to Proba, at www.newadvent.org/fathers/1102130.htm (accessed 23.08.2021), and a shortened version of the letter can be found at www.crossroadsinitiative.com/media/articles/ourfatheronthelordsprayer/ (accessed 23.08.2021).

'Midnight prayer'   This prayer is, of course, based on Jesus' parable about a man coming to his friend at midnight begging for bread (Luke 11.5–13), which follows immediately on Jesus' instruction to the disciples to pray the Lord's Prayer. He goes on to assure them of the responsiveness of his Abba God to their petitions.

'When we ask'   A riff on Luke 11.9–13, which follows straight on from the parable about the man at midnight and is, in the context of Luke's Gospel, all part of the wider commentary on the Lord's Prayer.

'Prayer against worrying'   This prayer, based on Jesus' teaching in Luke 12.22–31, expands the sense of praying in trust and dependence on God for the provision of all our needs.

'The bread of tomorrow'   There has long been speculation and debate about the best way to translate the rare biblical word *epiousios*, usually rendered as 'daily', and some have suggested that it is better translated as 'bread of [or for] tomorrow'. For a helpful (and brief) discussion of the various possibilities of translation, see Cherry, *Thy Will Be Done*, chapter 15.

'Daily manna'   This prayer draws on the story in Exodus 16 of the Israelites wandering in the wilderness, who complain to Moses that they will die of hunger, and then are supplied with daily manna falling from heaven (but not on the Sabbath – double is provided on the day preceding the Sabbath), as well as quails every evening (the quails somehow didn't make it into the prayer, perhaps in sympathy with vegetarians!).

'Yeast' and 'No yeast'   These two poems were written in the first lockdown in the UK, in March 2020, when various foodstuffs, including yeast, disappeared from supermarket shelves for weeks at a time, as anxious shoppers stockpiled – or, in this instance, tried out home baking as a way of making good use of all the additional time on their hands.

'Making soda bread in the blue kitchen'   This poem is in honour and loving memory of Evelyn Ross, a friend from London days who was a fine weaver and who died after many years of a rare degenerative illness during lockdown, so that it was only possible to attend her funeral online.

'Prayers for harvest (1)' The quotation 'all in the end is harvest' is from Edith Sitwell's poem 'Eurydice', and forms the second part of a couplet, 'Love is not changed by Death and nothing is lost; all in the end is harvest.' See Edith Sitwell, *Collected Poems* (London: Macmillan, 1979), p. 269.

'Prayer of the commode' This is very largely a 'found prayer' taken from some words of Kathleen Norris in her account of caring for her husband as he was dying of lung cancer, in *Acedia & Me: A Marriage, Monks and A Writer's Life* (New York: Riverhead Books, 2008), chapter 12. I was particularly struck by her phrase 'the comedy of grace', in the context of attentiveness to the most basic bodily needs, not only for food, clothing and shelter, but also for evacuation of human waste. She writes: 'my most "spiritual" activity during the last year of my husband's life was cleaning out his urinals and commodes' (p. 229). Such comedic attention to the body's waste is incorporated within our prayer for 'daily bread'; no part of human life is too mean to be acknowledged in our prayer. Perhaps this becomes more obvious to us, the older we get and the sicker we get, as our bodies begin to fail us and require of us deeper love and care.

Chapter 5 Forgive Us, As We Forgive

For a brief discussion of feminist analysis of sin, see my *Faith and Feminism: An Introduction to Christian Feminist Theology* (London: Darton, Longman & Todd, 2003), chapter 4. Valerie Saiving's oft-quoted 1960 essay is 'The Human Situation: A Feminine View', reprinted in Judith Plaskow and Carol P. Christ (eds), *Womanspirit Rising: A Feminist Reader in Religion* (San Francisco: Harper & Row, 1979), pp. 25–42.

For a recent, helpful discussion of the dangers of an emphasis on forgiveness for survivors of violence or trauma, see Esther McIntosh, 'The Trauma of Mothers: Motherhood, Violent

Crime and the Christian Motif of Forgiveness', in *Feminist Trauma Theologies: Body, Scripture and Church in Critical Perspective*, edited by Karen O'Donnell and Katie Cross (London: SCM Press, 2020), pp. 266–89. There has been a great deal of discussion recently about shame, and a proposal by some that the category of 'shame' is more resonant for many contemporary persons than that of sin. See, for example, Stephen Pattison, *Saving Face: Enfacement, Shame, Theology* (London: Routledge, 2013) and Judith Rossall, *Forbidden Fruit and Fig Leaves: Reading the Bible with the Shamed* (London: SCM Press, 2020).

'Confession for gender justice' This confession was written for a liturgy at the end of a Gender Study Day co-hosted by Queen's and WATCH (Women and the Church), in October 2012 at which Canon Lucy Winkett was the keynote speaker.

'A confession for returning' This was written on one of a number of holidays in south-west Cork, on the Sheep's Head Peninsula, an area of Ireland we have come to love and whose footpaths seem to be very much 'old ways' we need and have forgotten to tread.

'Confession for a lack of passion' I wrote this long before our recent experience of Covid, so it is interesting that the confession ends with a reference to 'the tight, sealed, scared place of lockdown' – which makes me wonder how far our global experience of lockdown has reduced our capacity to feel and dream and engendered in us a cautious, fearful approach that may diminish our humanity even as it keeps us safe.

Chapter 6 Lead Us Not Into Temptation, But Deliver Us From Evil

For more on the political context within which Jesus and the earliest Christians were living, see Crossan, *The Greatest Prayer*, chapter 8.

'To obtain and possess the kingdoms ...', Crossan, p. 173.

'Deliver us from evil' This prayer is a largely verbatim rendering of some words of Evelyn Underhill from her book on the Lord's Prayer, *Abba* (London: Longmans, Green & Co., 1940), pp. 76, 77, 82.

'Grenfell Tower lament' It is hardly likely that any British reader will need the context of this lament explained, but it is possible that readers elsewhere may do. On 14 June 2017, a fire broke out in the 24-storey Grenfell Tower block of flats in Kensington, London, and spread rapidly due to the building's inferior cladding. It cost the lives of 72 people, leading to a public inquiry and an independent review of building regulations and fire safety.

'A litany of struggle and remembrance' This has been set for three voices and congregational responses in bold but could be adapted for more voices or a single voice with responses. It is probably more effective with several voices, however.

Chapter 7 Prayers From The Desert

Yushi Nomura's translation of the sayings and stories from the desert abbas and ammas, with an introduction by Henri J. M. Nouwen, is published as *Desert Wisdom: Sayings from the Desert Fathers* (Maryknoll, NY: Orbis, 2001). I am grateful to Sr Benedicta Ward for her writings on the desert tradition (e.g. *The Desert Fathers: Sayings of the Early Christian Monks*, London: Penguin, revised edn, 2003; *Harlots of the Desert: A Study of Repentance in Early Monastic Sources*, Kalamazoo, MI: Liturgical Press, 1987) and for lectures she gave over a number of years to students on the Christian Spirituality course co-taught by Stephen Burns and myself at Queen's in the 1990s, which deepened my own engagement with the desert abbas and ammas.

For helpful accounts of the desert abbas and ammas, see John Chryssavgis, *In the Heart of the Desert: The Spirituality of the Desert Fathers and Mothers* (Bloomington, IN: World Wisdom, revised edn, 2008), Mary C. Earle, *The Desert*

Mothers: Practical Spiritual Wisdom for Every Day (London: SPCK, 2007), Mary Forman, *Praying with the Desert Mothers* (Collegeville, MN: Liturgical Press, 2005) and Benedicta Ward, as above.

'Arriving'   The last line of this prayer is a reference to Abba Agathon, who was said to have carried a pebble around in his mouth until he learned to be silent, *Desert Wisdom*, p. 5.

'To be set alight'   Based on a story of Abba Lot visiting Abba Joseph, *Desert Wisdom*, p. 92.

'To assist a sister or brother'   Based on a saying of Abba Poemen, *Desert Wisdom*, p. 17.

'Abiding in the cell'   Based on Abba Moses' saying: 'Go and sit in your cell, and your cell will teach you everything', *Desert Wisdom*, p. 14.

'To bear fruit'   *Desert Wisdom*, p. 40.

'Prayer for simplicity'   Based on a saying of Abba Hieracus, *Desert Wisdom*, p. 39.

'Those who hurt us'   Based on a saying of Abba Nilus, *Desert Wisdom*, p. 94.

'Rising, falling' and 'The daily round'   Based on a saying of Abba Sisoes, https://atlantaoratory.wordpress.com/2017/02/28/falling-down-and-getting-up/.

'The grief that is useful'   Based on a saying of Amma Syncletica, currently not traceable.

'Knowing when to speak'   Based on sayings by Abba Pambo, Abba Isidore of Pelusia, Abba Poeman, *Desert Wisdom*, pp. 76, 82–3 and 58.

'Love without judgement'   Based on a saying of Abba Xanthias, *Desert Wisdom*, p. 67.

'Prayer for patience'   Based on a saying of Amma Syncletica, *Desert Wisdom*, p. 19.

'This day's labour'   Based on a saying of Abba Elias, *Desert Wisdom*, p. 60.

'For a hard heart'   Based on a saying of Abba Poemen, *Desert Wisdom*, p. 59

'To keep God's commandments'   Based on a story about Abba Moses, *Desert Wisdom*, p. 9.

'A teachable spirit'   Based on a saying by Abba Isaiah, *Desert Wisdom*, p. 10.

'To accept the human lot'   Based on a story about John the Little, *Desert Wisdom*, pp. 12–13.

'To be delivered from folly'   Based on a saying of Abba Anthony, *Desert Wisdom*, p. 15.

'Prayer against the weariness of words'   Based on the story about Abba Agathon, *Desert Wisdom*, p. 5.

'Prayer against the weariness of others'   Based on Jeremiah 9.2, Song of Solomon 2.14 and Psalm 61.2.

'The well in the wilderness'   Based on an Egyptian saying, thirteenth century BCE, in Barbara Greene and Victor Gollancz, *God of a Hundred Names* (London: Hodder & Stoughton, 1962), p. 235.

Chapter 8 Canticle of the Creatures

Jen Hadfield's wonderful, horsey version of the Lord's Prayer, 'Paternoster', is in *Nigh-no-place* (Newcastle: Bloodaxe, 2008), p. 27.

St Francis of Assisi's 'Canticle of the Creatures' is widely known and available in a variety of versions in *Celebrating Common Prayer*, pp. 530–33 and online at www.oremus.org/liturgy/

ccp/14cants.html, numbers 63A and B; and in numerous other places, including http://franciscanseculars.com/the-canticle-of-the-creatures/ (accessed 27.08.2021).

'The donkey's prayer' This prayer was written during Holy Week 2020 when, for the first time in my life, churches were closed, due to the Covid pandemic, and Holy Week and Easter had to be marked privately in people's homes and online rather than as we would habitually do by gathering in person in the communities to which we belong:

'The primroses' prayer' This prayer quotes freely from Christopher Smart's long poem 'Jubilate Agno', well known in particular for extolling the virtues of Smart's cat, Jeoffrey, but also containing lines about the flowers and their worship of God, most of which can be found in Fragment B of the text, which is available online in a number of places, including Penn Arts and Sciences at the University of Pennsylvania: www.sas.upenn.edu/~cavitch/pdf-library?Smart_Jubilate.pdf (accessed 1.07.2021).

'The road to the isles' This poem, and the remaining three of the chapter, are evocations and celebrations of places that have come to mean much to me. Although I didn't get to Iona until well on in my life, it holds a deep place in my being. I was privileged to lead a retreat at the Abbey in Holy Week 2016 and to preach on Easter Sunday (the sermon is available as a download at www.ionabooks.com/product/easter-sunday-sermon-from-iona-abbey-pdf-download/ and in Neil Paynter, *The Sun Slowly Rises: Readings, Reflections and Prayers for Holy Week from the Iona Community* (Glasgow: Wild Goose, 2017), p. 119–23). In June 2017, Rosie Miles and I co-led a writing workshop at the MacLeod Centre, 'Writing body and soul', when it is possible I wrote this poem (I can't quite remember!).

'Aldeburgh' For many years during the 1990s and early 2000s, Aldeburgh was a place of regular pilgrimage, not least for the fabulous annual poetry festival every November, which was one of the best in the British Isles, and also for the wonderful music of Snape Maltings. The mudflats, endless pebble ridges and grey, cold seascapes of the east coast could not be more different from the land and seascapes of my native Devon, and it took me a long time to grow to love the very different topography of the Suffolk coast, but over years it has got under my skin and I would not be without it.

'Sunday morning at the abbey' For a longer number of years, I have been returning to Malling Abbey and, while there have been many changes over those years and the enclosed community of nuns is much smaller than it was when I first started going, it remains for me a place of anchor, homecoming and profound embrace.

'Our mother mountain' As noted above, my partner and I have discovered south-west Cork over a number of recent years and have had four or five stays in this most beautiful part of the world, three of them on the remote Sheep's Head Peninsula.

Chapter 9 For Yours Is The Kindom, The Power and The Glory

'The kindom, the power and the glory' This prayer is a largely verbatim rendering of some words of Evelyn Underhill from her book *Abba*, pp. 83–4, 87.

'Prayer for radical trust' Over many years, Donald Eadie has accompanied me as a spiritual companion and guide, and I owe much to his gentle wisdom.

'Seeking the face of God' This prayer takes its cue from Emily Dickinson's poem no. 257, from the story of God hiding Moses in the cleft of the rock as God passes by, in Exodus 33 and from the Song of Songs 2.14.

'Welcome, death' As for many, the experience of living with and through the pandemic has brought death a lot closer – not in a macabre way, but in a heightened awareness of how close we all live to death, something our ancestors would not have needed reminding of. As it happens, the writing of this book has coincided with a number of deaths in my immediate family and this has somehow brought my own death closer too. In this poem, she is a strapping country lass, sometimes shrouded in her thick winter cloak, who strides the Devon lanes and comes to invigorate, rather than diminish, the time I have left to me.

'Coming to you' All Saints' Church, Tudeley, on the outskirts of Tonbridge, Kent, is a small parish church with an extraordinary set of Chagall stained-glass windows. The East window was originally commissioned by Sir Henry and Lady d'Avigdor-Goldsmid as a memorial to their daughter, Sarah, who died in a sailing accident in 1963, aged 21. While Chagall was initially reluctant to take on the commission, when he finally accepted it and came to the church, he promptly offered to do all the remaining eleven windows. See www.tudeley. org/chagallwindows.htm and related webpages. My poem is particularly focused on the East window, which has various images relating to Sarah d'Avigdor-Goldsmid's death.

'Potting out the sunflower' The chapter and the whole book ends by returning to the daily and to Abba Poemen's saying about Abba Pior that every single day he made a fresh beginning. *Desert Wisdom*, p. 1.

Index of Titles